310 Nights At

Anchor

(and holding)

Andrew Dalby

This book is dedicated to my grandchildren

Oliver William Crothers
and
Megan Kathy Dalby

About the Author

Andrew Dalby is a British musician, composer, writer, and graduate of the Welsh College of Music and Drama in Cardiff. Born in North Yorkshire in 1962 he learnt to play the trumpet and after college spent twelve years as a school teacher, later becoming a self-employed musician. Amongst his many achievements he has taught scores of individuals to play musical instruments, is the founder of the Thirsk and District Royal British Legion Brass Band (which he started with a few friends in 1985) and has composed a number of works including a string quartet, a viola concerto, a Requiem Mass and many songs as well as a number of short pieces for brass band. He has two grown up children and a grandchild by each. He now lives aboard the sailing yacht "Drumlin" with his wife Claire on the west coast of Scotland.

Answers

I'm looking for some answers
To things I need to know.
I don't know what the question is,
So how can wisdom grow?

Life is full of mystery
And wonders to the mind,
But in my quest for meaning
No answers can I find.

Men can work with atoms
And split them into two,
Or see the farthest universe,
And haul it into view.

Yet when we turn to look inside
And view the world within,
Our eyes are strangely blinded.
By what? Our fear? Our sin?

Perhaps the question we should ask
Is not how do things work?
But why do hearts so freely break,
Why souls in torment hurt!

Maybe, as we in search of truth
Strive hard to learn life's meaning,
We have the answer all along,
When true to one's own feelings.

Andrew Dalby 19th July 2009

Preface

Having completed my first book *373 Days Afloat (and counting)* it soon became apparent that it would leave a question on the lips of my readers, "Is this new way of life as good as we expected?" It is one thing to take a risk and change one's life, but there is always a danger that it could be a disappointment or even a downright mistake.

310 Nights At Anchor (and holding) is an account of roughly a year in our present way of life and describes the realities faced by a couple who have chosen to live aboard a sailing yacht all year round, and it seeks to show the advantages and challenges of a semi nomadic life on the periphery of modern society. Although the sequel and natural counterpart to *373 Days Afloat,* which chronicles our escape from a suburban life to one of adventure at sea, it is hoped that this work will stand in its own right as it shines a light on an alternative way of living. In writing this book I wanted to share our experiences to illustrate how we have been able to take more control of our lives and gain greater freedom and independence; if anyone who honours me by reading this is entertained, encouraged, inspired, or helped to bring about meaningful change in their own lives I will consider my endeavour to have been worthwhile.

The text is essentially an edited version of the daily diary that we have kept and begins where *373 Days Afloat* finished. The structure of the book is mainly determined by where we were and what we were doing, but the narrative does divide into reasonably distinct sections giving a basis for the demarcation of the chapters. Where the diary is being quoted, it is printed in italics. In addition the text is interspersed with other information, observations, comments and quotations, and includes some of my own poetry and "philosophical" thoughts perhaps pretentiously entitled aphorisms which appear randomly dispersed throughout with no obvious context other than that they occur on the days these thoughts came to me!

This account of our voyage is also of interest as we were sailing in some of the same locations that Boswell, Johnson and Mairie Hedderwick had written about in their books *"A Journey to the Western Islands of Scotland and The Journal of a Tour to the Hebrides"* and *"Sea Change"* respectively; I read both during this trip. A visit to a place is more thrilling when one is observing something, or standing where, someone else has either fairly recently or across a span of nearly two centuries. One feels a connection and affinity with those fellow travellers. I urge you to read both of these excellent pieces of literature.

My reason for self-publishing this work is that if this is worthy of being available to anyone who would wish to read it then this book should be accessible! I do not expect that my readers will always agree with my ideas or opinions, but I do hope to provoke thoughtful consideration of them in an age when nonconformity is increasingly viewed with suspicion and even hostility. Today we live in a society where people are too comfortable to critically evaluate and challenge the status quo, and are often blind to, or unconcerned about the subtle erosion of their rights and liberties, or too afraid to speak out and stand up to the State for the follies and injustices it commits in our name.

I would like to thank to my wife Claire, for her help, support and encouragement in writing this book and for her help in keeping the journal upon which this is based.

Andrew Dalby, Dingwall, 2016

Aphorism

Growth causes poverty. When one individual entity grows it
takes from those around it. Like a plant depletes the
soil, so in economics a concentration of wealth
in one place means impoverishment
elsewhere. The logical conclusion
of growth is collapse as the
edifice consumes its
own foundations.

Andrew Dalby, 2nd November 2015

CHAPTER ONE

The End of the Beginning

"Now this is not the end. It is not even the
beginning of the end. But it is,
perhaps, the end of the
beginning." [1]
Sir Winston Churchill

It was 14 months since we had bought our sailing yacht Drumlin, and on 13th September 2013 we finally sailed her into Troon marina having completed our first full summer as seafaring nomads. We had experienced all four seasons as residents in our tiny ship. From that point on most of what we would do in the future would be familiar, part of our new normality. Our metamorphosis was complete! We had lived the caterpillar life working hard and growing fat in suburbia; we had survived the chrysalis process of lifestyle change and escaped the cocoon of domesticity; we had fled the rat race; and, like fee spirits, we had taken our first unsteady flight on butterfly wings unfettered by the usual cares of life. And now summer was drawing to its close and the time had come to hibernate...

After spending last winter afloat here in Troon on the Ayrshire coast and a further six months at sea, Drumlin was in need a of a little care and attention, the sort that only can be properly given in the relatively civilised surroundings of a good marina with access to a chandlery and "facilities". The first, and any yachtsman's least favourite, job was to strip the sea toilet down, decalcify the pipe work and replace the diaphragm in the pump. This is a malodorous task at best, and on most boats has to be tackled in the confined space of the heads. Like many do-it-yourself jobs the first time one attempts it there is a steep learning curve, and I have found it useful to keep a maintenance log book in which I record information about which tools were used and any tricks of the trade I learnt along the way, so that in future such jobs will be less onerous undertakings. It is also a useful way to make sure that routine servicing is completed on time and any small defects can be spotted early and preventative measures taken before costly repairs become necessary.

Another awkward job that we needed to address was checking and clearing the bilges. Previous experience taught us that the very lowest part of Drumlin's hull was prone to collecting dirty water which we have since concluded is what drains off the chain every time we weigh anchor. It just so happens that this lowest point is right in the middle of the saloon under the table which is firmly bolted through the floor to the keel support structure. Drumlin's floor is made of several large pieces of veneered marine plywood and to lift this requires the removal of the table even if you only want to see into the bilges. Having dismantled it all once before, this task was no longer such a puzzle and I decided that a simple cut made to one of the floor panels would enable it to be lifted without having to take out the table. This turned out to be a very successful modification.

In the summer months when sailing we need to be fastidious about bilge management because when Drumlin heels under sail any water in there has a nasty habit of seeping up through the cracks between the floor boards and wetting the carpet. Now at this point I would like to publicly put on record my unreserved apology to Chip and Bracken, our canine sailing companions, for wrongfully accusing them of creating the wet patch the first time we experienced this phenomenon! They are innocent of any wrong doing – at least on this occasion. It is also good to keep as much water out of the inside as possible, after all this is the primary function of a boat, indeed the definition of one, but in winter this will also help to reduce the moisture content in the atmosphere which just adds to the condensation.

A question that I am sure has arisen in the minds of fellow sailors is why do we not use a bilge pump? The answer is simply that the bilge pump we have, which has both manual and automatic switches, although functioning perfectly, does not become sufficiently submerged to pump out the relatively small amounts of water concerned. Drumlin's Bilges are probably no more than 6 inches (15cm) deep below the floor boards, not enough to activate the float switch (which is not set in the deepest position either) and certainly not enough to cover the extraction pipe to the pump. In short, if we were taking on significant amounts of water then the pump would work, and if we were aboard, we would probably see the problem coming through the floor before we heard the pump come on.

Last winter we found that the addition of a small 80W electric tube radiator similar to those beloved by gardeners with green houses, had made the forepeak (bedroom) much warmer and less prone to condensation. Given how economical they are to run we decided that we would fit another one, this time at the far end of the boat in the quarter berth (back bedroom). This too is part of our strategy to reduce condensation which can be quite a problem in the colder months. Very quickly, as the autumn advanced and the thermometer dropped outside, we began to feel warmer inside and saw less condensation.

In the summer months life aboard a boat is spent largely on deck, and it is fair to say that we enjoy twice as many square metres of room to roam than we do in winter when confined below. Winter has the potential to become cramped and claustrophobic, so we decided that some sort of tent to shelter the cockpit would allow us to continue to use this space. An hour or two of discussion with Claire, the taking of measurements and drawing plans resulted in the necessary specifications to present to a local sail maker who agreed to make our tent. Although this was not a cheap commission at £300, it was to be professionally made from the same material as lorry curtains, so we were confident it could cope with all that a Scottish winter could throw at it, and it gave us an extra "room".

-oOo-

By Sunday 22nd September we had now been in Troon for 9 days. The jobs on Drumlin's to-do list was growing at roughly the same rate as we were ticking them off, but progress was being made, and today the summer was determined to eke out her latter days by granting us sunshine to the very end. But drama is never very far away...

It was late in the afternoon, it was comfortably warm, and the sun was shining. Quite a lot of people were aboard their boats, many enjoying the pleasantly sunny weather and one of the last weekends of the season, sitting in the cockpits of their boats. There was a leisurely hum of activity all around the marina. Suddenly the tranquillity was broken when a man came running down the pontoon and disappeared into the office. Moments later the marina manager came in the opposite direction clearly on a mission. Minutes later the fire brigade and an ambulance arrived, and soon the pontoon was host to a several figures apparelled in full breathing apparatus and fireproof clothing all heading towards "Beatrice" a yacht near the far end of the pontoon. In typical British fashion

4

everyone remained aboard their boats stoically pretending that nothing out of the ordinary was happening each of us content in the knowledge that the experts were in charge of the situation. After the initial commotion had calmed down and a decent period of calm had prevailed, the chief fireman casually visited each boat with a crew aboard to explain confidentially that poor "Beatrice" had suffered a fire as the result of a gas fitting failure on the cooker. He politely suggested that we should all take reasonable steps to satisfy ourselves that our own gas systems were up to standard and properly serviced. To be honest we felt chastened as our cooker was the original and the flames burned with a sooty yellow flame and turned our pans black. We knew ours needed changing and so another item was added to the to-do list.

September gave way to October and the procession of jobs both great and small continued; each one filling as much time as was available to it. The main priority was to remove the sails and stow them along with the cloth dodgers that skirt the cockpit to protect us from spray when sailing. This is a job for a dry day so that nothing wet is able to fester over winter in the dark recesses of the cockpit locker. The other job for dry days is the continual round of putting teak oil onto the exterior woodwork and varnishing the companionway surround. This is a chore that always seems to catch up with me as winter approaches, not surprisingly during summer when conditions are perfect for this work; they are also perfect for sailing or sunbathing.

One part of Drumlin that we had not had to investigate closely was the navigation light fittings at the top of the mast. This happy state of affairs was, however, at an end because at some stage during our summer voyage something happened to the light structure that left it broken and twisted like a squashed top hat on a hobo's head. I had to climb the mast! In theory going up the mast is not a difficult activity because we have special steps riveted to the side of the mast rather like a series of stirrups. I donned my lifejacket, which has an integral safety harness, and clipped on to the main halyard, the rope that pulls the main sail up the mast; I tied a rope to my waist attached to a bucket containing the tools I thought I might need and began to climb. Meanwhile Claire took up the slack and ensured I was at all times securely belayed in the event I should lose my footing and fall. Not having a good head for heights I also took one further precaution, I put on my reading glasses so that I could not see clearly further than 3 feet in front of me rendering me blind to the altitude. It worked! The only thing that I hadn't counted on was the pendulum effect. The smallest amount of rocking on deck is hardly perceptible, but by the time you have reached the cross trees any movement becomes significant, and by the time you are looking down on the mast from above, the swaying is alarming. Matters were not helped 3 quarters of the way up when my bucket of tools snagged on the standing rigging and I had to ask Claire to disentangle it. Totally unaware of the increased amount of amplitude experienced at this level, she nimbly sprang out of the cockpit, gambolled along the starboard deck and began tugging at the offending pail incognisant of the sudden onset of terror I was experiencing as the mast began to lurch from side to side like a giant metronome. I clung to the pole, screwed my eyes tight shut and waited for equilibrium to be restored.

It turned out that I didn't need any tools. The whole of the light fitting which contains two lamps, one for the anchor light and the other for the three coloured navigation light, simply unclips leaving the electrical connections attached to the base plate. I returned to earth wobbly legged and perspiring. I made out that it was a hard climb, but I was kidding no one that it was anything but pure fear!

Ultimately it took a few months to source another light fitting as it was now an obsolete type. All the modern ones have a different attachment to the base plate, but fortunately a local boat electrical specialist found one for us and our lights were finally repaired, but I did make one small modification. I replaced the old incandescent anchor lamp with an L.E.D. array that is brighter and uses a fraction of the battery's power. This proved to be another very sensible decision.

-oOo-

I had toyed with the idea of turning our diary into some sort of book and as the days became cooler and the nights lengthened I began reviewing our log book and started the long process of writing what was to become *373 Days Afloat*. The memories of our new life were still recent and fresh, but it was quite astonishing to discover that incidents that we thought had happened at a particular time or in a certain place had become distorted and misremembered. The factual testimony of our log book served to remedy our errors and also recover some of the recollections that were slowly sinking into the quicksand of forgetfulness. The mind can play funny tricks even after such a short space of time. I sometimes wonder just how reliable many of us really are as witnesses to events if we do not accurately make records at the time! In addition to this the diary kept on reminding us of the problems we had faced and provoked us to think about how we would anticipate and overcome them the future. This resulted in my sudden new found fascination for cookery!

It has to be said that on a scale of 1 to 10 for good fortune in catering, I score about 11 because Claire is a fabulous cook.

She can conjure up the tastiest meals from the most unlikely ingredients in the blink of an eye, and although I can fend for myself and do cook, I am quite outclassed by her. Nevertheless, food and provisions can be a problem when out in the wilds between Scottish islands, just as it was for those seafaring explorers of old setting out across oceans into the unknown. So far we have managed to avoid Black Death, cholera or scurvy unlike the ancients, but a healthy diet of fresh food can be a challenge to acquire. The biggest problem is keeping food cold and meat is something we cannot store except in tins. Bread has a habit of going mouldy after a few days, as do cakes and pies. I was made to realise that perhaps our life was like life had been decades ago before our modern conveniences and I was moved to write the following at the end of *373 Days Afloat*:

> "Today people take fresh food for granted because it can be stored for longer and obtained easily. Our new life has made both of these conveniences harder to achieve. To address this problem I asked myself one simple question, "What would Grandma have done?" In days gone by food that would quickly perish was made at the time it was needed from storable ingredients. Simple staples such as flour, sugar, margarine and eggs can soon be turned into cakes, pancakes, scones and pastry. Fresh vegetables, pickles and preserves add colour and flavour to meals, and of course some tinned foods are necessary

in our circumstances. Simplifying the weekly shop has made it cheaper, perhaps healthier and certainly less difficult to procure what we require. All it has taken is the resolve to cook differently." [2]

The solution to our provisioning problem was really quite simple; we needed to obtain our food in kit form rather than pre assembled!

Ever since I was a child I have enjoyed watching the process of food preparation. In my infancy my mother would pull a chair up to the kitchen table for me to stand on and give me a piece of pastry to roll from which I made jam tarts out of the dough I had kneaded and made grey with my grubby little hands. I love to watch Claire bake, but one small chink seemed to me to appear in her armour one day as the winter storms began to jostle Drumlin making us unstable on our feet. At the best of times a still and level surface on a boat is not guaranteed, but on this occasion as I had observed a number of times before, Claire was struggling to make her modern electronic scales work. This again focused my attention on the Achilles' heel of the modern era; technology! Claire weighs her ingredients. This is quite normal and is nothing unusual, but today, in this situation, it was letting her down. Nature was having the last word! This made me think even harder about how baking was accomplished before modern conveniences. "What would Grandma have done?" I came to my second "revelation", proportions, instead of using weights; do as the Americans do, cook by ratios.

In my quest to simplify life I embraced a straight forward philosophy which I set out at the end of *373 Days Afloat*:

"A number of years ago I discovered the ideas of the Greek Philosopher Antisthenes (c. 445–365 BCE), who was the founder of cynicism, ... The goal of life is to be happy and this is achieved by being the best we can be (arête). To do this requires a positive mental attitude along with five other key qualities:

Minimalism; it is important to keep things as simple as possible.

Unashamed; it is vital to banish the most damaging emotion of all which is guilt and shame. ...

Self-reliant; we need to cultivate independence. ...

In tune with nature; ...

Critical thinking; ...

Predictably for me, and you may have already noticed from the list above, I have reduced this to a simple mnemonic, which by a happy coincidence for a musician like myself, is MUSIC! Here is my philosophy for life:

Try to be the best you can be through the positive pursuit of MUSIC!" [3]

In order to be more self-reliant we had to overcome problems which normal modern life uses technology to solve, but which in our situation would be inappropriate.

"To be a philosopher is ... to solve some of the problems of life, not only theoretically, but practically." [4]
Henry David Thoreau

Sure, we *could* have a fridge or even a freezer aboard, indeed, one of our cruising friends even has a washing machine on his yacht, but this would defeat some of our philosophical goals. Technology is reliant on fuel and would make us more dependent upon resources from "civilisation"; is less "green" causing us to be out of tune with nature; would involve bringing more things aboard Drumlin and would not be minimalistic. In fact, to do any of the above would, for us, be a negative step likely to bring less rather than greater satisfaction or happiness. In short, it is this kind of thing that represents what is ensnaring and pernicious about modern life. Think about it, you work hard and these labour saving devices and modern conveniences allow you a little time extra at night to relax and unwind. All this expensive technology saves you so much time freeing you up to work those ever longer hours to pay for them!

"I am wont to think that men are not so much the keepers
of herds as herds are the keepers of men, the
former are so much the freer." [5]
Henry David Thoreau

The food problem was in many ways solved. We knew that
next year we would have to make more food "in the field"
from storable ingredients (staples), but for me this was not
enough. Claire could make food this way due to her many
years of practice and, frankly, encyclopaedic memory for
things like recipes and food ideas. Now I can knock up quick
spaghetti bolognaise or full English breakfast, but baking was
another matter. Yes I can follow a recipe book, but that is not
self-reliant enough for me. I needed to understand how
cooking and baking works, to reduce this complicated art
form to manageable facts and distil it into an essence that I
could understand and, more importantly, use. I began my
research, which mainly consisted of pestering Claire for basic
recipes, rifling through her handwritten recipe book, dipping
into the few selected cookery books we have aboard and
trawling the internet. Bringing all the most useful recipes
together and making what essentially amounted to a shopping
list I began to see a pattern emerging. I had, what was for me,
a eureka moment, an Archimedean insight, just like in the
cartoons when a light comes on, the penny dropped. At this
point I apologise to any cooks, chefs, bakers, housewives and
Mum's reading this, as what I have discovered is probably
well known and blindingly obvious to such as you, but for me
this was a wonderful moment which actually has changed the
way I think about food and how I shop for it! The realisation
is that most recipes are a mixture of some or all of 4 types of
ingredient; fats, fluids, flour and sugar!

Spurred on by my discovery I began experimenting. First of all, I needed a way to measure so that I could use ratios or proportions to combine my ingredients. It seemed to me that any recipe could easily be translated into proportions, for example 800 grams of flour and 400 grams of sugar would be a 2:1 ratio. The problem arose with eggs! Clearly tackling some recipes flour and sugar first left the eggs a mystery, and then I saw it. On the shelf beside the locker where Claire keeps herbs, spices and condiments I saw a plastic shot glass! A small egg sized container that would be about full if the contents of an average egg (chicken not emu obviously) was to be cracked into it. Now I had my unit of measurement. From here on it was plain sailing. Using an egg sized measure any recipe could be made with nothing more than simple kitchen utensils. (See Appendix)

A Baker's Rhyme

Yorkshire puddings and pancakes too,
Are just a simple matter,
Flour and eggs in equal parts,
And milk to make the batter.

Dumplings and pastry are easy to make,
Two parts flour to one part fat,
A dash of water, give salt a shake,
And baking powder, unless rolled flat!

Six to two of flour and milk,
For scones, with one part marg,
And sugar OR cheese, just one part,
Then roll it thick and large.

Now cake's a doddle your pardon to beg
Mix all together with just one egg

Two parts of each is what to do
Flour and marg, some sugar too.

As for biscuits; flour, marg and sugar,
In proportion four to three then two,
Now add some flavour, a pinch of bi-carb,
Perhaps some oats, whate'er suits you!

Andrew Dalby, Troon, 3rd March 2014

-oOo-

We love our dogs, Chip and Bracken. In fact we love all animals with, perhaps in Claire's case, the exception of spiders. Animals make the world a better place, but dogs rightfully have earned the title of man's best friend! No matter what the world has thrown at you, no matter how bad you may be feeling, no matter how completely people let you down, a dog will always be there to greet you when you arrive home with its wagging tail and bucket loads of unconditional love. I was once told of an experiment we can do to prove that a dog is a man's best friend; lock your dog and your wife in a shed for an hour and see which one is most pleased to see you when you let them out! This obviously is a joke and NOT to be attempted, but it does make the point rather eloquently.

Two noteworthy incidents occurred in this month of October 2013. On the 14th Claire and I left the dogs at home whilst we went to the supermarket on our weekly shopping trip. I had used rather a lot of our supply of ingredients conducting baking experiments! Bracken, being a beagle and a rescued one at that, has a penchant for theft, so anything remotely edible has to be cleared away. We made a slight mistake and forgot to fully close one of the sliding locker doors. On our return we discovered Chip, the dog with a conscience and knowledge of right from wrong, trying his hardest to become invisible, and Bracken half way through devouring a litre bottle of cooking oil on the carpet. Had we entered him into a dog show he would have won a gold rosette for the dog with the shiniest coat, if nothing in the obedience category. Consequently we had to buy a new carpet for the saloon, but as with many setbacks there was a benefit to be derived from this. Earlier we had modified the floor panels to gain easier access the bilges; fitting a new carpet allowed us to cut it in a way that made lifting it less of a struggle when accessing under the floor, and rendering the whole process more straightforward too.

Aphorism

No one has authority over another save
that which the latter concedes to the
former, or the former takes by
the use or threat of force.

Andrew Dalby 16th October 2013

The other animal related incident happened 3 days later on the 17th and involved a seagull which we named Sally. On the boat moored beside us we noticed an unusual shape on the foredeck by the anchor locker. On closer inspection we saw it was a young seagull and it appeared injured. I took an old towel out with me and approached her from behind so as not to intimidate her. She was clearly not well and unable to make her escape. I laid the towel over her and carefully gathered her up and placed her in a large plastic storage box. At first we suspected a broken left wing but it did not have the appearance of a fracture, however, there was some red beneath that we could not properly see. We decided to take her to the local vetinary practice. We were greeted with a slight amount of bemusement, but were shown into the surgeon's consulting room whereupon she examined Sally. The red mark which we had suspected was blood turned out to be paint or some such pigment. Sally was clearly injured and our best guess was that in the night she had flown into the rigging of one of the yachts and crashed onto the deck. Unable to be set free the vet suggested that she be handed over to a local animal sanctuary that had the resources to nurse her back to health, so we handed her over to their care and that is the last we heard about Sally. We offered to pay for the consultation, but the vet said that they did not charge people who bring in wild animals for treatment.

-oOo-

It is a good idea to lift your boat out of the water every year to inspect the hull, remove any unwanted adherents, service the through hull fittings and anode as required and repaint the anti fouling paint. The 25th October was the day we had booked for the hoist, and ahead of us lay a week of hard work scrubbing and painting before we were to head off to Yorkshire on our annual pilgrimage to the dentist, optician and accountant; but on the positive side we would be visiting family and friends too.

We were pleasantly surprised at the good condition of everything down below and we quickly began preparing for the new coat of paint. One small detail lacking on Drumlin was a boot line, the thin strip of coloured paint that acts as a margin between the underwater anti-foul paint and the topside of the hull. We decided that a 5cm band above the present waterline would be perfect so we began the process of masking off ready to paint. We soon ran out of tape and I made a quick dash around the boat yard to the chandlery to buy more. Once inside I saw a cooker on the shop floor with a price tag on it. £200! Instantly my curiosity was aroused and I asked what was wrong with it. Given that it was just under half the price of a new one, I was naturally cautious, but there was nothing wrong with it, it was just second hand. It had been bought new the season before and lightly used only to be replaced recently by a more sophisticated model. After the tragedy of "Beatrice" a few weeks earlier, and in the knowledge that our cooker was really well past its useful service life, I'd have been a fool not to buy it there and then, so I did.

As is so often the case in the world of do-it-yourself what should be a simple job rarely is! The slim new cooker did not fit into the gimbals for the old one, they were too wide. I now had a real dilemma. I could not remove the old gimbals without rendering it impossible to put them back. If I failed to fit the new cooker, we would be without one at all! There was nothing for it, the old one really wasn't safe and I had an idea which called for a little improvisation. I soon drew up a plan to make a new set of mounts for our shiny new stainless steel kitchen appliance to take pride of place in the galley where once the old yellow enamelled stalwart had hung for 29 years, latterly, forlornly wheezing and belching out carbon monoxide fumes from its cool, jaundiced, smoke laden flames.

Soon the work was done, boot lines painted and anti-foul applied, and we were locking up and heading for the railway station for our trip south.

Aphorism

If we were to think about money in the same terms as we
do our food, we would waste less, consume less, and
only stockpile reasonable amounts. Greed would
be viewed like gluttony and society would
deplore the fat for their excess. As it is
we celebrate excess, encourage
greed and admire the
bloated.

Andrew Dalby 30th October 2013

CHAPTER TWO

Keeping It All in Perspective

"... and, lo, the star, which they saw in
the east, went before them ..." [6]

Like all migratory animals we finally had to answer nature's summons and begin the annual journey south for winter, not in search of a warmer climate, though instinctively that is what we would like to do, but to seek lodgings in the town of our origins. For us there was to be plenty of room, not in an inn, not even a stable, but a hayloft, the repurposed and eponymously named dwelling that was our daughter Hannah's 1 bedroom attic flat above a hair dressing salon on the corner of a busy street. After spending so long in the confined but cosy womb like interior of Drumlin suddenly to find ourselves in what most people would consider a particularly bijou flat was a strange experience. We felt vulnerable, even exposed by the relatively large void particularly above us when lying in bed staring up at the ceiling. To be honest it wasn't anything as romantic as the call of the wild or natural instinct that brought us back to Thirsk. Like that couple in ancient times it was principally the dictates of the State that made it necessary to return "home" to see our accountant and submit returns to the Inland Revenue. We also had appointments with the optician and dentist. Fun times ahead! There were added bonuses on this trip, however, as we were close enough to Scarborough to visit my father Malcolm, and our son and daughter in law Martin and Lisa, and to catch up with many old friends and neighbours around the area. Soon the time had come to return to Troon and to launch Drumlin.

"And it came to pass in those days, that there went out
a decree from Caesar Augustus that all the
world should be taxed ... And all
went to be taxed, everyone
into his own city." [7]

We returned home on the last day of November in time for Drumlin's lift in at 11.00 am on Wednesday 4th December 2013. The hoist was booked; we had vacated Drumlin with the 2 dogs and ... disaster! Just as the behemoth which is the hoist approached Drumlin and began to line up to straddle her hull, there was a catastrophic failure of one of its hydraulic lines rendering this Goliath of a machine more impotent than a superhero exposed to kryptonite! Fortunately Drumlin was not in the hoist when this happened as then we would have been completely homeless! What should have been a 30 minute exercise took several hours as an engineer had to be brought in to fix the plant before we could go anywhere. Later in the day an engineer arrived and repaired the offending component and the sleeping giant was roused to its task and Drumlin was placed back into her natural environment.

The 5th of December 2013 distinguished itself in a couple of memorable ways. First of all Great Britain, like all the other countries facing the North Sea and the Baltic, was subjected to the elemental ferocity of hurricane Xavier! Yesterday, the 4th December, an explosive cyclogenesis occurred to the south of Greenland and, as it travelled eastwards over Scotland to Norway on the 5th, it deepened causing hurricane force winds and the most serious North Sea tidal surge in over 30 years. Chaos ensued all over the United Kingdom and abroad with travel disruption and floods damaging homes and businesses. Aboard Drumlin in the marina the wind was of such strength even early in the day that Claire likened the noise to the sound of a Boeing 747 airliner taking off. It was as if the storm was nature's sudden outpouring of grief at what was today's second tragedy, the passing of perhaps one of the greatest men in modern history, Nelson Rolihlahla Mandela (18th July 1918 – 5th December 2013). I cannot write anything about this man which has not been said more eloquently a thousand times before. He stands as a shining example of mankind's ability to stand up against tyranny in all its forms without compromising one's own integrity, and he stands as an example to all on how to manage conflict, how to be reconciled with the past and one's old adversary, and how to move forward together. Nelson Mandela leaves this world a better place than when he entered it and the whole of the human race owes him a great debt.

Friday 13th December (appropriately enough) terrorised us again with a severe wind forecast from the Met Office, which proved to be no idle threat because Saturday 14th delivered the promised south westerly force 9 – 11 winds! The rest of December was spent pottering with the ordinary affairs of life which included taking delivery of the bespoke tent I had designed to put over the boom to enclose the cockpit and effectively create a 3rd room, and making preparations for Christmas and New Year. We were going to spend Christmas in Scarborough with Martin and Lisa and then drive to Inverness to spend Hogmanay with Claire's family. In order to do this Claire had first to go by train to Inverness to pick up her Father's spare car which she did on Wednesday 18th returning home the following day in blizzard conditions.

By Friday 20th December we were, once again, thrust back into, what is for the vast majority, "normal" life probably too soon after our previous and recent incursion, and I began to feel the toxicity of modern existence gradually polluting my mind again. A sense of the gradual and unstoppable immersion into the shallow frivolities of today's consumerist lifestyle grew within me and I began to rebel. Don't misunderstand me, I was very happy to be spending time with my family and friends, it was just this all pervasive choking smog of the Christmas festival hijacked by consumerism that was asphyxiating me. The whole of December had been a slow crescendo towards the fortissimo of the final days of 2013, and naturally I had to purge my mind and soul of its infectious poison; the consequence was the following poetic trilogy calling for a re-evaluation of these precious few December days in the Christian calendar.

Just like those wise men three

You give your gifts at Christmas, just like those wise men three,
All wrapped in good intentions, those parcels, bombs may be!
Pardoned for all your meanness, thus from your guilt set free.

Be careful what you wish for! That baby Jesus, He
Would not have said to Santa, "Inflict those things on me!"
You give your gifts at Christmas, just like those wise men three.

Gold's eternal light of Heav'n. "Wise man you'd make of me?"
Your gilt-y gift at Christmas, "A king you'd have me be!"
Pardoned for all your meanness, and from your guilt set free.

Terpene tears of frankincense, boswellia shed for thee,
Your fragrant gift at Christmas, bled prayers to ask of me.
You give your gifts at Christmas, just like those wise men three.

"Mortician's myrrh you give me? Embalming oil? For me?
There is such joy in giving, this ev'ry one can see!"
Pardoned for all your meanness, and from your guilt set free.

So are the gifts you offer a sinner's guilty plea?
Or are those contributions just compensatory?
You give your gifts at Christmas, just like those wise men
three.
Pardoned for all your meanness? And from your guilt, set
free?

Andrew Dalby, Scarborough, 29th December 2013

-oOo-

It's not about the Saviour

We give our gifts at Christmas just like those wise men three,
To fete the birth of Jesus, we decorate a tree.
We buy our gifts at Christmas, and spend to please our
friends,
For fear they'll be offended, and thus we start the trend.
We must maintain at Christmas appearance, we can't be lax,
We have to do our duty, and pay this Yuletide tax.

It's not about the Saviour, the child sent to be king,
It's all a great big guilt trip, with distinctly hollow ring.
It's not about redemption, from sin by Christ set free,
It's all about pure business, the cash economy.
It's not about the shepherds, hark this herald angel sings,
"It's all about the sheep, who follow those three kings."

The pressure's on from every side, to buy and give and swap
and smile,
To over eat and over spend, that makes this season vile.

If I don't buy a present, to give to you and you,
And spend for sake of spending, what else am I to do?
Let's claim it back for that small babe, His poor nativity,
And celebrate with conscience clear... No presents, please, for
me.

Andrew Dalby, Dingwall, 3rd January 2014

-oOo-

Is this what Christmas means to you?

Those three wise men or were they kings?
Gave THAT poor child those precious things,
And now we're taught to be polite
That we should follow this holy rite.

Now were they wise those monarchs three,
This stick to give Christianity?

For now the troubled and the poor,
Inside the Christian merchant's door,
Are made to spend their riches few!
Is this what Christmas means to you?

Let's put the meaning back in Christmas,
Be worthy of The Lamb, [8]
And give our time, our love, our selves,
Lest Christmas be a sham.

For now the poor give to the rich,
Peasants, gifts to kings!
At Christmas time we sacrifice,
To commerce, offerings.

Would it not be brightest and best,
To give these presents a well earned rest?

Andrew Dalby Dingwall 3rd January 2014

These three poems were written over the course of Christmas 2013 and I know I shall be unpopular with some people for saying these things, but say them I must! I am sure I shall be misunderstood, particularly by those who don't like what I have to say.

"Pythagoras was misunderstood, and Socrates, and Jesus,
and
Luther, and Copernicus, and Galileo, and Newton, and
every pure and wise spirit that ever took flesh.
To be great is to be misunderstood." [9]
Ralph Waldo Emerson

I now live a life of self imposed austerity with little spare cash. I am not complaining, it is just a fact and there are many people in similar circumstances for varying reasons. Then along comes Christmas with its implicit expectation that everyone parties, buys presents and sends each other cards. A forced and false season of merriment marketed and advertised to fever pitch by the media with promises that this or that toy, tool, technological gadget or new piece of furniture will be the answer to satisfy all our needs and wants; and that this or that food retailer is the means by which we will avoid social disaster when we entertain our guests.

"You need not rest your reputation
on the dinners you give." [10]
Henry David Thoreau

25

We are made to feel that we must compete to be the best and are made to feel guilty or inadequate if we do not keep up. So, buy now and pay later, and boy do we pay for it!

Children are exposed to images of a big, red faced, jolly and rotund Santa, a role model of excess, frivolity and intemperance; or some cold, smiling, strangely dressed inanimate snowman benignly coming to life to carry them off at the dead of night. This is the stuff of nightmares and these would be characters of horror in any other context! Then perhaps, if we are vigilant, we might just see pictures or dioramas of a nativity scene with a bright clean stable, with angels, animals, kings and shepherds adoring a baby held in the arms of a beatific Virgin Mary, when the reality was probably more likely to have been squalor and extreme discomfort for all concerned. And we dress it all up in consumerism, false promises and tinsel, played out to a sound track of tacky, sentimental, sugar coated music.

I shall be called a kill joy and compared with Charles Dickens' Scrooge, but I would rather give a gift when it is needed, or receive one that is given with love than merely give or receive just because that is what is expected. It is because of personal and corporate greed, and our culture of consumerism, that we have lost sight of what Christmas means; and if we have or profess no religion, why do we bother anyway? Surely then Christmas should be irrelevant! I am all for celebrating Christmas if that means contemplating God's love for mankind, the joy of a child's birth and the warmth of family and friendship, but let us just do it simply, for little cost and keep an eye on the real meaning of Christmas. **Remember, Jesus came to pay our debt, not to get us into it!**

Andrew Dalby, Troon, 4th January 2014

-oOo-

Friday 3rd of January 2014 saw us home in Troon after the festivities were over and my thoughts turned once again to practical tasks on Drumlin, such as lengthening our anchor chain and servicing the engine, and Claire's to celebrating her 50th Birthday in March! By the 7th she had booked the most expensive hotel in town and sent out invitations to the party.

Friday 10th January 2014, Troon, Overcast and Heavy Rain, Day 451:

Today two things have been in the news, both of them concerning politicians, the so called "Plebgate" scandal and the French President.

Firstly: the "Plebgate" scandal concerns The Right Honourable Andrew Mitchell, Conservative Member of Parliament for the Royal town of Sutton Coalfield, who allegedly had an altercation with police officers outside Downing Street on 19th September 2012 which has today resulted in Police Constable Keith Wallis pleading guilty at the Old Bailey to lying in a statement that he made. Now what bothers me about this is nothing to do with the trial or those involved, but rather the fact that the Metropolitan Police Commissioner Sir Bernard Hogan-Howe has felt it necessary to apologise. Yes it is unfortunate that police officers under his command have been unprofessional, and one has committed a crime, and that a Member of Parliament lost his temper. So what? The institutions associated were not involved. The Metropolitan Police did nothing wrong, individuals did. This apologising, falling on swords and calling for resignations is childish. Grow up people! If your colleagues screw up, deal with the individuals; unless there is an institutional system failure, keep your mouths shut!

27

Secondly: the French President François Hollande has allegedly been caught having an affair. Again, so what? The French generally do not seem to care. I don't care.

These people are only human just like the rest of us; we should not expect more or less of them than we would of our car mechanic, window cleaner, bus driver or green grocer. Let's have some common sense and proportion here and not require anything more of these people than we as individuals would expect in our own lives. Would you call for your family doctor or dentist to resign if he had an affair with a consenting adult or if your church pastor or postman swore at a jobsworth policeman? Furthermore, would we expect the secretary of State for health to apologise for the doctor's actions or the Archbishop of Canterbury to resign because of the behaviour of your pastor? No! When will people who work in the media, and who flatter themselves that they can hold people in public office to account on our behalf, start to ask sensible questions on issues that really matter instead of indulging in mischief making and petty point scoring?

Saturday 11th January 2014, Troon, NW2 Sunny/Cold, Day 452:

I serviced the outboard motor for the dinghy; it has been running unevenly and using a lot of fuel.

Wednesday 15th January 2014, Troon, Rain, Day456:

We bought charts for the area around the Isle of Skye, a 2014 nautical Almanac and oil to service Drumlins inboard engine from the chandlery today and our daughter in law Lisa passed her final exams today for her Pharmacy qualifications. We are so proud of her, especially as she is following in Claire's footsteps.

Saturday 18th January 2014, Troon, E3 Overcast, Day 459:

The main task today was to service the main engine which involves complete chaos both inside and outside of the boat. Access to the engine is gained via 2 routes, the cockpit locker which is normally replete with general sailing paraphernalia, and the steps that grant access in and out of the saloon.

Unlike changing the oil in your car which is usually done in a garage up on a ramp so the engineer can access the sump plug on the bottom of the engine to drop the oil out under the influence of gravity, a yacht's oil change is conducted in the living room, and because the engine is mounted very low in the boat the oil has to be sucked up through the dip stick hole using a syringe – No honestly, I am not kidding. Oil changes on a boat are tricky affairs fraught with opportunities to have a major ecological disaster in the comfort of your own home!

Tuesday 28th January 2014, Troon, E2 Fair, Day 469:

I have finally brought together all the parts of my book 373 Days Afloat (and counting) in one complete document for editing, tweaking, proofreading and formatting.

Friday 31st January 2014, Troon, SE6-7 Overcast, Day 472:

Last year before setting sail we bought 2 large 25 litre water carriers. This ensured that we always had a back up supply of drinking water, but I made a mistake in having such large containers because they are difficult to carry to and from Drumlin in the dinghy. For this reason I decided to buy 2 smaller 10 litre water carriers. Experience has taught us that a little and often is a better strategy than big, heavy and infrequently!

February was a month of storms and lulls, and between the tempests I spent my time treating Drumlin's external woodwork with teak oil and doing general maintenance duties. Low pressure on the barometer is usually an indication that there will be bad weather and on Saturday 1st the glass read 962 millibars and a week later on the 8th it plummeted to 952, the lowest pressure we had seen since we came aboard Drumlin!

Wednesday 5th February turned out to be one of those frustrating days trying to solve a simple problem. Although we do not need to use the 12 volt electrical system very much during the winter months because we are connected to the mains electricity supply, we do use it occasionally in the forepeak (bedroom) as that is the only light source in there. We periodically switch on the battery charger, a great monster of a device installed when the boat was built in the bowels of the cockpit locker, to keep the batteries in good condition whilst they lay fallow for 6 months. I mention this because we had noticed, despite our conscientious periodic charging, that the lights were becoming dim! Something was wrong. I opened up the battery locker and measured the voltage across each battery, or rather the lack of it. I switched on the battery charger and measured again; no change. The battery charger, although working, was not sending any current to the batteries. I fought my way through the clutter in the cockpit locker to the battery charger to find out if there was any charge emanating from it, a simple matter one would think, but no!

One of the most oft repeated words I hear these days when talking to people, especially about technology (and computers in particular), is the word "upgrade". Drumlin has been upgraded in many ways. We tend to think of an upgrade as being an improvement, a small add on that increases value or convenience of some sort. At the risk of being unfairly branded a Luddite I want to suggest that this word "upgrade" should in many cases be treated with a great deal of caution, even perhaps replaced with the word "downgrade". I am sure that the original designer of Drumlin, naval architect Laurent Giles, had he felt it necessary, would have put in a hot and cold pressurised water system with shower, and, being the genius he was, would not have installed it precisely so as to deny access to the battery charger! What is more, we hardly ever use the pressurised water system; we mainly use the original foot pump for cold water. This brings me neatly to the two points I want to make; firstly, the "upgrade" has not improved matters concerning the maintenance and repair of the electrical system; and secondly, the "upgraded" water system is entirely unnecessary, we don't use it! I am sure that most readers may initially think it is illogical not to use such an "improvement", after all hot and cold running water is a necessity. Is it? Think about it for a moment. Using a tap that runs continuously unless turned off wastes water, having hot water in a tank takes energy to heat it up, and it eventually goes cold. When we are at sea we cannot afford to waste water; we would have to put into a marina every week just to replenish it. On the other hand, if we are in a marina every week why would we need the hot pressurised water which is only appropriate for showering when we could use the marina's facilities? Trust me on this, you do not *need* a shower; a sponge and a bowl of water achieve the same results, use less fuel, and conserve precious water supplies. We now have the absurd situation that we have both a battery charger and a water system aboard taking up space and are entirely useless. Fortunately the batteries do charge when the engine is running and in summer this is entirely sufficient. In winter I now use a regular car battery charger to top them up.

Anchoring is a subject that is of great interest to us, especially as our way of life and safety rely upon it for 6 months of each year. Drumlin has a good 35lb CQR anchor and 40 metres of chain which is for most purposes adequate, but this year we are planning to venture further afield into the more remote extremities of the Hebrides and the pilot books recommend extra chain. The usual practice of anchoring involves putting the anchor on the sea bed and laying out chain behind it to a length of anywhere between 4 and 10 times the maximum depth of water expected depending on conditions. Providing that you manage to dig the anchor in this will normally suffice, however, a skipper must do all due diligence to ensure a watch is kept and the anchor does not drag or break lose. The general rule is that more chain is better (given enough room for the yacht to swing without colliding with anything or running aground); after all chain is useless in the locker! I prefer to calculate how much chain to lay using another formula than the 4 to 10 times maximum depth, I put out as much chain as I can and double check that it is at least 12 times as much as the square root of the maximum depth of water; it always seems to work!

Another little trick we do is to tandem anchor. We carry a separate length of chain 10 metres long and a smaller 15lb CQR kedge anchor. This is added to the end of the anchor chain where the main anchor is attached and is laid out first. NB IT IS NOT ATTACHED TO THE CROWN OF THE MAIN ANCHOR! Admittedly laying two anchors is a little tricky, and retrieving them even harder, but if set correctly will hold very well. I always attach a tripping line to the small anchor, it aids in its retrieval.

Despite having good ground tackle in which we have great confidence we decided to beef up our armoury with two additions, the first was an additional 20 metres of chain and the second was to obtain an angel! At this point I must tell anyone who doesn't speak nautical that an angel is not, in this case, a celestial being, but simply a weight to put on the anchor chain (placed near the bows) to keep more chain in contact with the seabed and reduce the likelihood of the anchor being dislodged. As a bonus it also has the effect of reducing the boat's swinging circle in calm weather. The problem I faced was where to get one. There are many examples in the yachting press and on the internet telling how people have made and improvised angels out of the carcasses of old car batteries filled with cement or recycling gym weights et cetera. I found my solution in an unexpected place on Wednesday 12th February when I was helping my cousin Paul with a little D.I.Y. at his house. A house brick! Not the small brown variety, but a large 440 x 215mm concrete block! He kindly drilled a hole in one end so I could attach a rope to it, and our anchoring system was at last complete. Not many weeks later all of this equipment was to be tried and tested, and it proved itself worthy of every inch of extra space it used.

During the first 3 weeks of February I had been working with my publisher, PublishNation, on the final edits and layout of my first book "373 Days Afloat (and counting)". By Friday 21st February they had sent me a copy of the book cover for approval. It was excellent! Everything was now in the hands of the publisher and on Thursday 27th the final edit of the book was submitted for publication. It is possible to keep tweaking and tinkering, but there comes a time when it is what it is and needs to be sent out into the world to live its own life. During that week of waiting I was at a loose end so I turned my attention to other projects. On Saturday 22nd I began my baking experiments. That evening I made 11 biscuits, 6 buns and 6 jam tarts, and Claire said they were yummy, but there is only so much baking one can do so inevitably I returned to my first love, music and by the evening of Sunday 23rd I finished my 4th consecutive Psalm setting for choir. Tuesday 25th saw me complete my 5th Psalm and another opus was born! [11]

The Scoundrel's Ridoubt

I never cease to marvel at those men
Who proudly boast they loy'ly serve their state,
And never once do raise a question when
Their nation's leaders tell them who to hate.

"I am a patriot," they boldly cry,
And hide behind a mask of false conceit,
But though they can't conceal the guilty lie,
That still small voice lays blame down at their feet. [12]

It is the scoundrel's only sure ridoubt,
The racist's castle; call it by its name!
For love of country, that's the moral drought,
They think they stand above those not the same.

So call yourself a patriot my friend,
But all you are is racist in the end!

Andrew Dalby Troon 27th February 2014

I was listening to an American drone pilot being interviewed on the radio in late 2013 and he was describing a typical day at work. He would drive from his suburban home in California to his Air Force Base about an hour away whereupon he would be briefed, then enter a room from which he would remotely fly a drone aircraft over Afghanistan. He was in direct contact with soldiers on the ground and involved in real time warfare engaging targets and killing them from half way around the globe. He explained how he could communicate with, and hear the fearful tense voices of his comrades under fire from the enemy, the native people in whose land his colleagues were an occupying force and obviously not universally welcome, and how he had to acquire, engage and destroy targets to protect his fellow Americans and allies. It was clear from the way he spoke that he was proud to serve his country in this way and he believed that what he was doing was justified, morally right and acceptable. He had no qualms about sending his children off to school in the morning, kissing his wife goodbye and going to work to maim and slaughter faceless human beings thousands of miles away then to return home at night to sleep safely and soundly in his own bed. I was reminded of the words of Samuel Johnson:

"Patriotism is the last refuge of the scoundrel." [13]

When doing the research necessary to put this book together I came across some work by the anarchist political philosopher Emma Goldman (1869 – 1940) and I have included some of her comments here. I strongly urge you to look up the website in the references and read the whole essay yourself. In her essay "Patriotism, A Menace to Liberty", 1911 she cites the Russian novelist Leo Tolstoy (1828 – 1910) as defining patriotism:

"...as the principle that will justify the training of
wholesale murderers; a trade that requires better equipment
for the exercise of man-killing than the making
of such necessities of life as shoes, clothing,
and houses; a trade that guarantees better
returns and greater glory than that of
the average workingman [sic]." [14]

She goes on to cite the French socialist politician Gustave Hervé (1871 – 1944):

"Patriotism ... is a superstition artificially created and
maintained through a network of lies and
falsehoods; a superstition that robs man
of his self-respect and dignity, and
increases his arrogance
and conceit." [15]

It is a disturbing fact that we are still encouraged to
consider the vile idea that there are people who are inferior
morally, religiously, politically, intellectually and (tacitly)
racially. It is an idea that contributed to the rise of Nazism and
fascism. These ideas continue to flourish in academia in that
some "experts" advocate the forced contact in the world's few
remaining rain forests and wildernesses of uncontacted tribes
who are unwilling to be assimilated. Ideas grounded in an
arrogant self image of particularly white Anglo Saxon Euro-
American westerners who innately, even instinctively, believe
that they are racially superior to the peoples of "less well
developed" societies. These ideas are alive and well and dress
themselves in the vestments of academic learning or
politically correct attitudes to disguise their atrocities as
foreign aid, conservation measures, missionary work, peace
keeping and the war on terror. Until we stop trying to impose
our ideas and values on other cultures and engage in
meaningful and respectful dialogue we will continue to
ferment discontent and cause irreparable harm. Until we begin
to listen and learn we will achieve nothing. Where other
nations do not share our values we should seek to understand
and persuade, even to allow difference. Rather than being
aggressive, we can refuse to trade; we can promote change by
refusing to engage with them. Frankly we need to grow up in
our dealings with unpalatable nations. We have learnt that we
should not smack our children, what's the difference?

March is a big month for birthdays in our family. The 1st is our daughter Hannah's (this year, 2014, she is 21 years old), the 26th is Claire's and the 31st is our son Martin's. It is also a month when the world begins to warm up and our thoughts of putting to sea return. It is always the case that there appears to be a backlog of tasks to perform before Drumlin is ready to sail and this month further teak oiling, varnishing and deck painting has been necessary, as has stowing our winter things and unpacking and bending on Drumlins sails and canvass work.

Between bouts of vigorous labour I continued my cooking experiments making quiches and pancakes. On Tuesday 4th the proof copy of *"373 Days Afloat (and counting)"* arrived. I was very happy with the quality of the end product I had spent so long working on. Three days later I ordered 10 more copies to send to family and friends which duly arrived on Monday 10th , the day after our daughter Hannah announced that she had resigned from her job and was moving to Carrickfergus in Northern Ireland to be with her partner Gareth.

We enjoyed a few days of respite from readying Drumlin for the season between Sunday 16th – Tuesday 18th March with our good friends Barbara and Trevor who came to Troon to see us. They are keen caravaners so it was natural thing to do to visit a local caravan dealership to feast our eyes on the beautiful homes from home mounted on trailers. Caravans and boats have a lot in common; both are moveable and in both one is at home once inside. They are also both symbols of freedom, not just freedom of movement, but freedom to reside where you arrive, not where you are tied. It seems to me that there is something deeply innate in the human condition which craves the freedom of new horizons whilst needing the security of a place to call home.

There's none so deaf as them as won't hear!

When warning bells ring clarion clear,
And toll as if to honour the dead,
There's none so deaf as them as won't hear!

I oft recall my old mother dear,
Those words she spoke with shake of her head,
When warning bells rang clarion clear!

There's fools down paths no sane man would steer,
And angel's feet would ne'er dare to tread;
There's none so deaf as them as won't hear!

With prophet's eyes the future is near,
But fools insist on pressing ahead;
When warning bells ring clarion clear.

I oft recall my old mother dear,
These words, this mantra, wearily said,
There's none so deaf as them as won't hear!

So heed the warnings, signs should be read,
Be wise, beware when all's done and said,
When warning bells ring clarion clear,
There's none so deaf as them as won't hear!

Andrew Dalby, Troon, Friday 21st March 2014.

We celebrated Claire's actual birthday (Wednesday 26th March) by draining the bilges of water and taking Drumlin out into the bay for a short shake down sail. Everything was fine except that I managed to break the key in the ignition; fortunately I was able to restart the engine and motor back into the marina. The following day I managed to have a new key cut in town, and thinking that all was well with life I returned home and decided to service the windlass, the winch that hauls up the anchor. The windlass is probably the only really necessary labour saving device aboard a sailing boat as anyone who has tried to pull an anchor and all of its chain aboard by hand will testify. They are also positioned in what is the most hostile environment for a machine; right on the bows where the sea washes salt water over it day after day. In addition to this, not to put too fine a point on a delicate subject, it is Chip and Bracken's favourite place to ... Well you work it out!

I have dismantled, cleaned and lubricated the windlass before and was well aware of the danger of losing pieces over the side if I was clumsy. I was clumsy! Lifting the gypsy off the spindle I was not careful enough to check to see if anything was stuck to the grease on the underside, and the clutch spacer was; temporarily! As if in slow motion, at the moment I turned the gypsy over to examine it, the spacer lost grip and flew over the side into 3 metres of soupy marina brine never to be seen again. As it was made of stainless steel there was no point in seeking out a strong magnet and going fishing. It was Thursday afternoon, where on earth was I going to find a replacement part for this one piece of absolutely vital machinery before Tuesday, the day we were due to put to sea? As it turned out to my absolute astonishment the maker of the windlass Simpson Lawrence was based in Paisley [16] 27 miles away, and a quick phone call established that they had the part I required, so my uncle Stewart who lives locally kindly took me there the following day to buy another. This turned out to be a fascinating shopping trip. The original company of Simpson Lawrence was based in the very area of Paisley I had to go to, but the business I was visiting had bought all of their old stock when Simpson Lawrence was taken over by a larger concern. The gentleman running this enterprise was an engineer and ex Simpson Lawrence employee, keen to continue selling the old company's products, and intent on not only continuing to supply spares, but to produce new winches and windlasses too. He was extremely knowledgeable about the equipment and, moreover, infectiously enthusiastic about his work. It is always a joy to meet someone who is so passionate about what they do, especially when they can convey that love and excitement to others and enthral them by their sheer energy. I came away not only bearing the part I needed, but frankly feeling better for being in his company for an hour!

Whilst I was away doing penance for my engineering sins, Claire was at home baking cakes for the party. She had decided that a birthday cake of adequate proportions would be too much to create in our small galley oven, so her master plan was to confect individual buns instead. Meanwhile family and friends were slowly gathering in Troon and checking in to their various places of accommodation and the party atmosphere was slowly fermenting. When I returned home I reassembled the windlass and took advantage of my Father in law's car to transport three month's worth of provisions from the local supermarket back to Drumlin. Victualling complete, we were just about ready to begin the summer season of sailing, and now it was time to party!

Saturday 29th March 2014, Troon, E3 Sunny Spells, Day 529:
All of our family and a number of friends descended on the Architect William Leiper's 1899 stately creation the Piersland House Hotel [17] opposite the Royal Troon golf course, one of

the host courses for the British Open Golf Championship, to celebrate Claire's 50th Birthday. We dined in the magnificent surroundings of what was once Sir Alexander Walker's old family home. Sir Alexander was the grandson of Johnnie Walker the Scotch whisky producer, but for me there was another piece of history much closer to home.

When I was a child we had a beautiful black Labrador sheepdog cross called Tess, and when I was about 4 years old I recall her digging a small pit under the flowering blackcurrant bush in the back garden of our Northallerton home and giving birth to her pups, much to my mother's consternation as she had tried repeatedly to encourage her to accomplish her confinement in the relative warmth and comfort of the outhouse. My maternal grandfather Reverend Harry Spencer, minister of the Clarkston Baptist Church in Glasgow throughout the 1960s to the early 1980s, was associated with the Christian Endeavour holiday home in Troon where he arranged for one of Tess's beautiful dog puppies to be homed. The dog's name was Bruce. He spent his long and happy life as a full time resident of what is now the Piersland House Hotel. I have a very fond childhood memory of a visit we made with Tess and Granddad to see Bruce. Bruce knew his mum, and Tess knew her son!

Sunday 30th March 2014, Troon, NE6-7 Sunny and Hazy, Day 530:
We spent Mothers day as a family again at the Piersland where we all enjoyed Sunday lunch before everyone had to begin their various long journeys home to both the Highlands and Yorkshire, and in Hannah's case, Carrickfergus in Northern Ireland to begin her new life over there.

CHAPTER THREE

A Rush to the Start

"Only a few more laps to go and then
the action will begin. Unless this
is the action, which it is." [18]
Murray Walker

It was our intention to explore north of Ardnamurchan point
this season so we were going to have to head for Tobermory
on the Isle of Mull as swiftly as possible. The implication of
this was that we would have to sail in a matter of a few weeks
over waters that we had taken all of last year to cover if we
were to make the most of our time in the north and have
sufficient time to return south for winter. There was,
therefore, quite an atmosphere of urgency...

We had intended setting off today, Tuesday April 1st, but
we had been so busy recently that we slept in! Feeling
appropriately foolish I went to the marina office to explain
why we had outstayed our welcome and to pay for our extra
day's berth as our contract ran out on 31st March. Stephen, the
manager, kindly waived any fees and therefore we can count
this night as our 142nd free night and 1st free night of this
season! The following morning we managed to sail from
Troon in what turned into a force 7 near gale which at one
point propelled us along at 7.3 knots with only a tiny amount
of jib out!

Lady Isle is a small rocky bird colony approximately 2
nautical miles west of Troon and as we passed by we saw our
first dolphin of the season. We were heading for
Campbeltown on the Mull of Kintyre, but as we entered the

Kilbrannan Sound to the west of Arran Claire went a funny shade of green; conditions were becoming interesting. It is a couple of miles down Campbeltown Loch from the open sea and given the lively and favourable wind direction we were able to sail right into the loch to our anchorage. The following day we rested as we were exhausted, but there was no likelihood of going anywhere as it was foggy. What was most gratifying, however, was to know how well Drumlin had coped in the worst weather we had so far sailed her in. She inspires confidence!

Five days later on Sunday 6th April I spent the day planning the trip around the Mull of Kintyre. Previously we had only returned into the Clyde round the Mull, we had not yet rounded it westwards. This is because last year we didn't go round, we went straight down to the Northern Irish coast and Glenarm, and on our return we came up on the west side, so in reality we had never attempted this passage. The question on our minds was whether to go through the inner sound or to go the long way round. We were considering setting off on Monday 7th April but when the day dawned the forecast was for westerly gale force winds and the times of the tides were not helpful. We delayed our departure. As predicted, the storm arrived at midnight, so we remained in our snug anchorage for a few more days. Surprisingly, given the challenging weather conditions, we noticed a few more yachts around as the week progressed; the Easter holiday had begun.

Pitter Patter Pours

Pitter patter pours percussive rain once more,
And choirs of clouds consort across the sky, while
Wind in whistles weaves counterpoint 'neath my door.

Droning dull and damp, the air chills through the score,
And fog's ensemble drapes around the band, while
Pitter patter pours percussive rain once more.

Fright'ning light'ning, flashes lyrics to the fore,
And thunder's clash is bass line in reply, while
Wind in whistles weaves counterpoint 'neath my door.

Ferocious fugues of flood carry all before,
And theme and countersubject drift on by, while
Pitter patter pours percussive rain once more,

Ice cold cantata canons onto the floor,
And rolls the drum that timeless hum of hail, while
Wind in whistles weaves counterpoint 'neath my door.

When the tempest's temp'rament is tuned, restored,
And orchestrates the summer, one last encor?
Pitter patter pours percussive rain once more,
Wind in whistles weaves counterpoint 'neath my door.

Andrew Dalby Campbeltown 9th April 2014

Friday 11th April 2014, Ardminish Bay Gigha, W4
Overcast Sky and Moderate Sea, Day 542:
We left Campbeltown at dawn and rounded the Mull of Kintyre and came north to Gigha. We managed to sail quite a lot of the way on the southward passage to the Mull and the northward one away from it but motored west through the sound itself to Macrihanish. Strong winds are forecast again for tomorrow.

(Bean Casserole Vegetables and Dumplings.)
Free Night 152/11

Monday 14th April 2014, Ardminish Bay, NW3 Sunny, Day 545:

Today we went ashore. My first objective was to find the shop. I am delighted to report that Gigha, as of last August following a 9 month period without one, now has a good, well stocked shop. Even fresh vegetables! Meat, bread and dairy were well catered for and staples and tinned goods in plentiful supply; even gas could be obtained with patience! I feel that Gigha is very fortunate not to have lost forever this vital focal point for the community. I am glad to be able to respond to my scathing criticism of Gigha given vent in my previous book "373 Days Afloat" and to say that I salute Gigha in going some way towards redeeming itself. I still stand by my criticism of the "selective" nature of tenancy on the island and the "rip off" tourist element to the local economy. To give an example, at the top of today's menu at one establishment was lobster at £52, the next dish £45, then £35 on the specials board. Did you know that they can live to be up to 60 years old in the wild? I would want a signed suicide note naming me personally as the beneficiary from the poor crustacean before I would pay that sort of money for a meal of lobster, or any other creature for that matter. I would rather pay WaterAid [19] to dig a couple of wells in Africa before stuffing my face on the remains of an unfortunate homarus gamarus which has been deprived of its life in order to help raise funds for the chef's next Ferrari or foreign holiday! Gigha functions again, but it still needs fixing!

The dogs enjoyed dragging me through the village after which I filled the pair of 10 litre water carriers. I decided that I would do a couple more trips ashore for water to finish topping up the water tank.

This time last year we were in Troon in sunshine and being pinned down and battered by gale and severe gale force southerly winds.

(Chile Con Veg)   *Free Night 155/14*

Tuesday 15th April 2014, Ardfern Lagoon, SE2-SW4-5 Sunny, Day 546:

The journey from Gigha to Ardfern was, from a sailing point of view, very unremarkable. Having left Gigha under sail in light winds we found ourselves not able to progress without resorting to the engine just north of the island. As usual Drumlin's power plant ticked along like a sewing machine. It wasn't until we were approaching the M[ac]Cormack Isles just outside Loch na Cille a couple of hours that I went below to write the log and mark the charts that I had a completely irrational sense that something was wrong. I checked the charts and the tidal calculations; everything was fine. We had done all our "pre-flight" checks, nothing had been overlooked. Still, something felt wrong! I lifted the engine cover which doubles as the step into Drumlin's saloon. There it was, the unmistakeable aroma of hot oil. I shone a light into the bottom of the engine compartment and there was the evidence; a slick of warm, black, shiny oil. Casually I told Claire that we were to alter course to go into Loch na Cille, a small and pretty inlet open to the south west and not ideal shelter in anything but the calmest of conditions.

"Why?" came the response from the helm.

"Never mind why, just do as I ask!"

"But why?"

There was no point in arguing, I had to tell her that we were in grave and imminent danger of a catastrophic engine failure. She complied, and turned at once!

Given the possibility that we were in real trouble if the engine did die on us we needed to be well anchored, so I rigged up the tandem anchor and we made sure that we were well and truly dug in. I then set to work on the engine. About half a litre of oil had dropped into the bilge beneath the engine and initially it appeared as if the seal on the sump had failed. In fact what had happened was that the oil pressure sensor which is on the side of the engine had begun to leak and oil was finding its way down and along the sump edge and finally dripping from the nuts that hold it in place. I refitted the sensor with some PTFE tape, cleaned out the spillage and topped up the engine with fresh oil. She started up without incident and the leak was repaired; cautiously we resumed our journey very relieved that the fault had been detected in time.

(Vegetable Curry and Rice)　　　　*Free Night 156/15*

Thursday 17th April 2014, Ardfern Lagoon, W5-8 Sunny Intervals, Day 548:
This time last year we were still being held up by bad weather in Troon and spent the day listening to Mrs Thatcher's funeral! Today Claire did some baking and I went ashore to find water.

In our quest for self-sufficiency and to preserve drinking water we have decided to use grey water sources for washing up. I went ashore to collect water from a stream and also to try my hand at foraging for wild plants. New nettles are abundant, but not to our taste, as are docks. I did manage to positively identify oenanthe crocata or water drop-wort, a relative of hemlock, and, according to Mr Maybe, [20] the number 1 cause of DEATH BY PLANT in the United Kingdom. So, last year having failed as a hunter, this year I do as a gatherer too. At least I survive to try again another day.

Other News: Our son Martin cut his finger at work and needed 3 stitches, and Claire, not to be out done, sliced her thumb when she was cooking. I saw a heron and heard my first cuckoo of the year.

(Casserole with soya and mash)   *Free Night 158/17*

Friday 18th April 2014, Ardfern Lagoon, S1-2 Sunny but Cool, Day 549:

I walked into the village with Chip to buy some bread and eggs from the shop then took to the dinghy to go exploring. I visited Eilean Dubh again where there is a wreck on the beach and some ruined buildings that I wanted to investigate further. Last year the vegetation was quite well established limiting access up the hillside. This year, being earlier in the spring, I managed to access the two structures which I estimated were about 3 by 4 metres and had an entrance. The walls appeared to have been deliberately constructed to allow air to pass between the dry stones and I saw nothing that appeared to me to represent a hearth. I wonder if they are perhaps storage or drying cleits? There is also a slightly larger pear shaped structure, perhaps a dwelling but I really could not be sure.

The ship I estimated to be about 12 metres long and what little remains of it shows no obvious signs of machinery and I suspect she was canoe ended. I looked for, but could not find any sign of a stern gland in the keel suggesting a propeller shaft, so my guess is that she is a vessel from the days of sail and if she did have an engine it would have been retro fitted and mounted obliquely through the hull like the Loch Fyne Skiffs were. She appears to have been beached with the stern / rudder end furthest up the beach. There is what looks like a large bracket, a piece of symmetrical iron work rather like a capital letter "R", which I interpreted as part of the rudder and there is evidence of flat iron strips on the ribs. She appears to be lying on her port side and I wonder if she had been destroyed by fire. All that remains of her is now covered at high water.

(Bean stew and dumplings)　　　　　*Free Night 159/18*

Saturday 19th April 2014, Ardfern Lagoon, S2-3 Sunny, Day 550:

I continued my exploration of the islands today this time going ashore on Eilean Mhic Chrion. Last year it was too overgrown to climb the steep hill, but this year I have better footwear and the greenery is not yet in full summer swing and I managed to scramble up the goat's tracks to the top of the middle summit. The view all round was excellent. I assume there are adders her as there is plenty of evidence of common lizards on which they prey. I saw lizards albeit briefly.

(Homemade Pizza)　　　　　*Free Night 160/19*

Monday 21st April 2014, Ardfern Lagoon, NE/E5-7 Sunny, Day 552:

If you stay in one place long enough you can see things that are not always apparent to the casual observer. Today I noticed an inflatable dinghy over on the island; it had been there for a very long time. It was getting dark and I could not see any sign of activity on the island, so I decided to row over and investigate. It isn't until you are several hundred yards away from your boat in what is rapidly descending into complete velvety darkness that you realise what a foolish undertaking paddling about in tiny boats at night is. However, I did justify my cavalier undertaking on the grounds that someone had to be on the island as the dinghy was unlikely to have arrived there of its own accord. When I reached the dinghy it was securely tied to the shore but nobody was around. I then noticed that one of the other yachts on one of the local moorings had someone aboard. I rowed over and hailed the occupant. A very charming gentleman appeared on deck and I apologised to him for disturbing him but was concerned about the owner of the dinghy on the island. It turned out to be his wife and she was ashore walking their dog. Satisfied that I had not "passed by on the other side" [21] I bade him a good night and returned to Drumlin with a clear conscience.

Tuesday 22nd April 2014, Horseshoe Bay Kerrera, E2-3 Showers, Day 553:
We left Ardfern at about half past 3 local time to get the north flowing tide for Oban. There was a brisk north easterly wind which allowed us to sail through the Dorus Mor once again, this time in the opposite direction. Fair winds continued and we also sailed through the Sound of Luing only resorting to the use of the engine as we turned northwest to leave the north end of the sound. We have made 3 steps on our journey to Tobermory now and have covered 139 nm in only 3 weeks and a large proportion of that has been under sail.

Other news - Martin rang this morning to say that his 8 year old budgie Hobbit died during the night.

(Vegetable Chile)   *Free Night 163/22*

I recorded this on my mobile phone:

We left Ardfern on Tuesday 22nd
April and sailed through the notorious
Dorus Mor and the Sound of Luing. 21

50

miles later we were snugly anchored in Horseshoe Bay in Kerrera Sound half a mile from Oban. We spent quite a lot of time here last year and it has been a treat to be reacquainted with the flock of wild goats on the island, all of whom appear fit and well and last year's kid has really grown up. We have also spotted the pair of buzzards that we observed nesting in the cliffs last year. So far the otter has not shown herself, but we are confident she is around here somewhere. It's like visiting old friends!

Wednesday 23rd April 2014, Horseshoe Bay, E/NE2-3 Overcast, Day 554:
I went ashore to the burn for some grey water and to walk the dogs, otherwise it has been a quiet day spent reading. Claire baked scones and made homemade tomato and lentil soup.

(Tuna Pasta)   *Free Night 164/23*

Sunday 27th April 2014, Horseshoe Bay, NE2 Sunny, Day 558:
It has been a beautiful day and we spent much of it reading. I made some scones (Part of my baking research!). This date last year was very similar spent in Millport, but the days either side were more unsettled.

(Bacon in Pasta)   *Free Night 168/27*

Tuesday 29th April 2014, Horseshoe Bay, NE 2 Cool and Sunny, Day 560:

It began cool and overcast, but as the day wore on the sun came out. I went ashore for more stream water and to walk the dogs, Claire made scones and we read. The plan is to stop here tomorrow and go to Inninmore Bay to overnight before heading up the Sound of Mull on Thursday assisted by the forecast force 5 easterly.

In the news today it was announced that a school teacher in Leeds, Ann Maguire, was stabbed and killed by one of her pupils weeks before she was due to retire.

(Tuna Pasta)   *Free Night 170/29*

Wednesday 30th April 2014, Inninmore Bay Morvern, ENE 4 Rain, Day 561:

We left Horseshoe Bay this morning and moored up at Cardingmill (Oban) where we walked the dogs then went to the supermarket to do a big stock up on provisions. It threw it down with rain and we got thoroughly soaked. At 3pm we set off for Innenmore Bay, our planned stop off point on our way to Tobermory. We saw this bay in use last year, and as it is sheltered from the west round to the south east through north, we thought it would be a suitable place to break our journey. It is! The wind was occasionally gusty over the top of the hill but on the whole the bay offers good shelter in these conditions. There is a bit of swell although it is not at all intolerable. During the night we were joined by a small fishing vessel, but she set off again at 6 am on the high tide.

(Vegetables with tomato and basil sauce and mash.)
Free Night 171/30

Thursday 1st May 2014, Tobermory, E3-4 Sunshine & Showers, Day 562:

It is a year ago that I made the decision to record "free nights" and so far we are piling them up. Anchoring is a good way to save £20.00 + per day!

This season I also resolved to try to save our precious drinking water and by extension reduce the need to call in at marinas and harbours by using grey water for washing up and bathing. We have a small 5 litre water carrier which I have been filling up in streams. This has made a CONSIDERABLE difference. Eg. Washing the day's dishes can consume as much as 3 litres of water, as much as 1 ½ days worth of drinking water for one person. Or to put it another way 4 days washing up reduces time at sea by nearly a week! It has proved worth the effort and so far we have not had to use any or our reserve water.

Our cruise up the Sound of Mull today, about 15 nm from Inninnmore Bay, was almost entirely completed under sail. We used 15 minutes of engine to weigh anchor and exit the bay, another 15 minutes of motoring to find our spot and cast our anchor. Even without the swarm of summer yachts the moorings themselves here in Tobermory give the appearance of crowding. The area allocated as an anchorage is a miserly sliver of water squeezed against the rocks with hardly room to swing a cat, much less anchor one [22]; although I have seen one do it last year! We are in 10 metres of water and due to the paucity of acreage we can only deploy 25 metres of chain! Any competent sailor will tell you that the minimum amount of chain should be equal to 4 times the maximum depth of water. Still the wind is not strong and it is fairly well sheltered so we shall see how we get on. We managed well last year.

Given that the Clyde Cruising Club Sailing Directions says that the Sound of Mull is the most heavily trafficked stretch of water in Scotland we had it virtually to ourselves today. Last year it was like a motorway of boats; today we saw perhaps 4 other yachts and less than a dozen commercial vessels.

(Vegetable Casserole & Dumplings) Free Night 172/31

"...Tober Morar [*Sic*]... appears to an unexperienced eye
formed for the security of ships." [23]
Samuel Johnson

"Tobermorie is an excellent harbour. An island
lies before it, and it is surrounded
by a hilly theatre." [24]
James Boswell

Tuesday 6th May 2014, Tobermory, SW4-5 Sunshine and Showers, Day 567:

I had been ashore today and I met the gentleman from a boat anchored near to us and had a chat with him. His boat, a Seamaster 2, was called *Soustray* and his name was George. He had some very good davits on the stern of his boat and I was curious where he had obtained them. He had made them himself. One thing led to another and we extended an invitation to come aboard for tea which he graciously accepted. The log book continues:-

George told us that he is a coppersmith by trade and he had worked on HMS Dreadnought, the United Kingdom's first nuclear powered submarine. He told us she was the first British submarine to surface at the North Pole on 3rd March 1971!

The 81 metre long 3,500 ton nuclear submarine HMS Dreadnaught S101 [25] was built in Barrow-in-Furness by Vickers Armstrongs between June 1959 and October 1960 at an estimated cost of £18,400,000 and, thanks in part to Admiral Mountbatten's good relations with the US Navy Chief of Operations Arleigh Burke and the 1958 UK-US Mutual Defence Agreement, she was powered by America's Westinghouse Electric Corporation's S5W reactor. Capable of making 20 knots surfaced and 28 knots submerged she carried a compliment of 113 crew and 24 torpedoes. After a successful career Dreadnaught left service in 1980 and is now laid up afloat waiting to be dismantled at Rosyth Dockyard on the Firth of Forth in Scotland. There are some campaigners who wish her to be returned to Barrow-in-Furness as a tourist attraction.

CHAPTER FOUR

Catching Up with the Past

"Nought was familiar but the heavens, from
under whose roof the voyager
never passes." [26]
Henry David Thoreau

Thursday 8th May 2014, Loch Caenn Traigh, Variable or
W2 Showers, Day 568:
*We were woken up this morning by the rumble of an
engine, and popping our heads out of the fore hatch revealed
the MV Discovery,* [27] *a 20,186GT, 168.74 metre long
passenger liner anchoring in Tobermory Bay. By 8am 4
lifeboats had been launched from the davits and the
passengers were being ferried ashore; to do what at such an
early hour we do not know!*

*At 9am we left Tobermory to head north around
Ardnamurchan Point. We are now in new waters! We
managed to sail a little part of the way but we probably
motored ¾ of the 24 nm which saw us safely into a very
beautiful anchorage.*

(Pasta and vegetables with Tomato and Basil sauce)
Free Night 179/38

Friday 9th May 2014, Loch Caenn Traigh, NW3-4
Sunshine and Showers, Day 570:
*Today has been a go nowhere day. There is a house above
us on the shore with a constantly running diesel generator.
How green is that? There is a persistent hum. Claire
discovered on the internet that the beach was used to practice*

for the D day landings with live fire! To this day ordnance
pops up on the beaches and has to be dealt with by the MOD.
These 2 facts inspired my sonnet!

Claire baked scones. Very nice!

Kentra Bay

We anchored in the peaceful Kentra bay,
Upon the north of Arndnamurchan's arm,
A place of beauty far from any fray,
A wilderness untouched by any harm.

But oh alas, this is so far from true,
The wee small house perched up above the loch,
Her noisy generator hid from view,
Exhales the fumes of diesel round the clock.

And of the white and sandy beach so fair,
That pristine broad expanse of silky strand,
What ill or evil could be lurking there,
To render this a piece of hostile land?

The bombs and bullets used to practise war
Left here, that's what, by those who came before!

Andrew Dalby, Kentra Bay, 9th May 2014

On 27 October 1941 Lord Louis Mountbatten replaced
Admiral of the Fleet Roger John Brownlow Keyes as Chief of
Combined Operations, a department of the British War Office
set up during Second World War to harass the Germans in
Europe by conducting raids by the use of combined military
forces. Keyes was removed because some of his plans were
considered impractical by the Chiefs of Staff.

Kentra Bay was used as a practice ground for some of the training of the 3 combined military services. One example I learnt about tells the story of 3 Hurricane aircraft of 516 Squadron RAF Connell which left their base on 6th February 1944 [28] as part of a training mission in Kentra Bay to act as hostiles against a training exercise for an amphibious landing. These exercises were so realistic that live ammunition was used, and not without cost as men really were killed and injured. History has revealed that this training was without doubt necessary as its efficacy was tried, tested and found invaluable on 6th June 1944 or D day as it is more commonly known. Today we often talk glibly about the numbers of casualties when studying military history, but it is worth noting that the 3 airmen on this occasion, having completed their mission were to lose their way in cloud and fog on the way back to base. They decided to split up and seek any airfield they could. W/O J E Stephen RAF (24) headed towards RAF Tiree, Flt Lt A J Woodgate RNZAF (21) attempted to fly low along the Sound of Mull and P/O Larry Figgis climbed above the cloud and eventually crash landed near Stirling. Stephen and Woodgate sadly failed to find safety and the wreckage of their aeroplanes was discovered a few days later. They were someone's sons, perhaps brothers or husbands – Lest we forget!

The Oban Times reported that on the 25th January 2012 on the beach at Kentra Bay, known as the Singing Sands, a number of World War II finned mortar bombs were found, probably uncovered after all these years by storms that had recently raged. As if to underscore this point, when Claire and I were in the museum at Arisaig a gentleman came in with a handful of unspent rifle bullets which he had picked up off the beach! We tend to think of the problem of unexploded ordnance as being one confined to places like northern France and Belgium, remnants of the First World War, but the fact is that the lethal detritus of war is everywhere, often where we might least expect it to be and still capable of maiming and killing innocent people long after the belligerents have gone home.

(Pasta, new potatoes and hotdogs in bolognaise sauce.)
Free Night 180/39

Sunday 11th May 2014, Loch Moidart, N3 Sunny & Broken Cloud, Day 572:
It is 13.00 hrs and I have spent a couple of hours in the dinghy exploring. It was low tide and I have finally earned my wings and can add to my credentials the title of Hunter Gather. Well gatherer, as today I finally, without anyone's help, found a good crop of mussels. They were quite well down the shore and only just above the water at low tide and we have just passed neaps. They are obviously untouched wild mussels as they are quite large and barnacle encrusted. I took 10 from one boulder and 10 from another. There were hundreds. If we do not make any more diary entries we have died of food poisoning! This will be:-
Free Meal 3

I forgot to mention that we have had the cockpit tent up and with the heavy showers we had yesterday and over night we have managed to fill our 5 litre grey water carrier. Result!

I also rowed over to Riksa Island. It appears to be an ancient, natural and largely untouched woodland with many deciduous trees and a lot of moss.

Apparently, according to Haswell Smith, the Castle Tioram which is Gaelic for dry or fair was the home of Ranald the son of Somerled, Lord of the Isles. [29]

I took Chip ashore at high tide this afternoon at about 4pm and I met a couple paddling back from the Castle Tioram island. They had not realised it was a tidal island. They also pointed out to me that there were two deer on the island. I took Chip back to Drumlin and went back to investigate. Capredus capredus, better known to most of us as roe deer, live in pairs or trios and not herds, and where they are not persecuted by man can be quite bold in his presence![30] This pair tolerated my approach to within about 30 metres. I managed to take some very special photographs. Nature has been kind to me today.

(Mussels)   *Free Night 182/41*

Monday 12th May 2014, Moidart, NE3 Cold & Rain, Day 573:

I have been struck by 3 things this morning; first the silence, we are so far from "civilisation" that noise is notable by its absence; second, there are very few fences here if you can overlook the castle! Oh, and a purely practical safety fence protecting the unwary from a precipitous drop beside the castle; and third, something Dr Johnson may have missed on his journey from Armadale to Coll, trees! Moidart enjoys a good range of arboreal variety, indeed Riska island is entirely and densely forested.

"There is no tree for either shelter or timber. The
oak and the thorn is equally a stranger, and
the whole country is extended in
uniform nakedness..." [31]
Samuel Johnson

Thanks to the rain today we managed to collect 10 litres of water!

(Soya Casserole with Mashed Potato) Free Night 183/42

Tuesday 13th May 2014, Moidart, W4 Sunny, Day 574:
It has been a very pleasant day. This morning I took Chip ashore for a good run, he didn't need to go on his lead, and I met a couple with an elderly sheep dog. We had a chat and I then met a couple who had owned a 27 feet long Yacht in their younger days. They'd taken up caravanning instead.

Afterwards I delivered Chip to Drumlin and rowed clockwise around Riska. I found 2 access points on the northwest and one on the east shore where I would take a small boat ashore; if it was my island! We spent the afternoon reading and I planned tomorrow's journey. We have decided, having initially discounted it, to go to Arisaig in Loch Nam Ceall, a convoluted but well marked entry into good shelter with facilities available. The alternative was Mallaig with its requirement to pay to park!

This full on westerly wind combined with the approaching spring tide is making us sway a little, but this has proved to be a secure anchorage.

(Chile con Soya Mince)   Free Night 184/43

Moidart Haiku

The silence makes deaf,
But for the bird song piercing;
So pure the spring air.

Andrew Dalby, Moidart, 13th May 2014

Wednesday 14th May 2014, Arisaig Loch Nan Ceall, S/SW4-5 Overcast, Day 575:
We had a good sail only using the jib, but still made 5 knots and more, up the Sound of Arisaig from Moidart. The entry into Loch Nan Ceall is a double bend, left then right; simple if you get it right! There are perches to aid navigation but the shallow depths, numerous rocks and sweeping currents make this the sort of passage that moistens the palms of your hands! Once inside it is very sheltered, full of yachts on moorings, and has an inviting shoreline by the village. We shall explore tomorrow weather permitting.

We have telephone and internet signal. This is good as being unable to keep tabs on children and other family becomes unnerving after a few days.

I have been thinking about my music and composing; I should regard it in 3 ways, music I write for others to perform, music I write for me to realise, and the music I can and should do for the sake of art. (That really means the sort of music not many people but music connoisseurs would appreciate!) As for the poetry, I need to explore some new themes...

(Tuna and Pasta)   *Free Night 185/44*

The Special Operations Executive (SOE) [32] was a highly secret British World War II organisation officially formed by the Minister of Economic Warfare Hugh Dalton on 22 July 1940. Its purpose was to spy on and sabotage the enemy, and to aid resistance in enemy occupied territories. Dalton and his successor, Major General Colin Gubbins, modelled the organisation along similar lines to those they had observed used by the Irish Republican Army (IRA)!

SOE was sometimes referred to as "the Baker Street Irregulars" because of the location of its London headquarters, but others have called it "Churchill's Secret Army" and those more squeamish dubbed it the "Ministry of Ungentlemanly Warfare", as if the rules, etiquette and niceties of cricket apply in war! SOE, however, was not so particular; causing disruption, unrest and assisting anti-establishment organisations in enemy territory were the order of the day. Furthermore, it was not fussy about who it employed so long as they were suited to the mission in hand; homosexuals (illegal at the time), criminals, communists, soldiers guilty of misconduct, men and women of any social class, in fact SOE was so far ahead of the attitudes prevailing at the time that it was even prepared to deploy women in armed combat! It is interesting to note that of the 13,000 people involved in SOE during the war, about 3,200 (24.6%) were women; two particularly famous examples were Odette Hallowes and Violette Szabo.

SOE requisitioned a number of country houses for its various activities, so much so that it became a joke that SOE stood for *"Stately 'omes of England"*. Agents received commando training by William E. Fairbairn and Eric A. Sykes at Arisaig House south east of the village in Lochaber and Inverailort Castle. Fairbairn and Sykes, former Inspectors in the Shanghai Municipal Police, are remembered today for inventing the F-S fighting knife, a particular type of double edged stiletto blade specifically designed for ease of concealment and penetration of an opponent's ribs. What a legacy!

After the war, on 15 January 1946, the Special Operations Executive was officially dissolved. There is a memorial in Arisaig village commemorating those men and women who served and died in SOE.

Whilst I was researching about the SOE I came across an interesting criticism of it which I include here for the reader's consideration: [33]

> The mode of warfare encouraged and promoted by SOE is considered by several modern commentators to have established the modern model that many alleged terrorist organisations emulate. [34]

> Two opposed views were quoted by Tony Geraghty in The Irish War: The Hidden Conflict Between the IRA and British Intelligence. M. R. D. Foot, who

wrote several official histories of SOE wrote:

"The Irish [thanks to the example set by Collins [35] and followed by the SOE] can thus claim that their resistance provide the originating impulse for resistance to tyrannies worse than any they had to endure themselves. And the Irish resistance as Collins led it, showed the rest of the world an economical way to fight wars the only sane way they can be fought in the age of the nuclear bomb."

However the British military historian John Keegan wrote:

"We must recognise that our response to the scourge of terrorism is compromised by what we did through SOE. The justification ... that we had no other means of striking back at the enemy ... is exactly the argument used by the Red Brigades, the Baader-Meinhoff gang, the PFLP, [36] the IRA and every other half-articulate terrorist organisation on Earth. Futile to argue that we were a democracy and Hitler a tyrant. Means besmirch ends. SOE besmirched Britain."

Friday 16th May 2014, Arisaig, S/SW4-8, Day 577:

It is fortunate that this morning, just after his children had gone to school, my friend Doug rang for a chat; fortunate because his call had me on my feet and looking out of the boat as I was talking to him. His call ended just after 10 am and no sooner had I hung up than the anchor broke out and we were dragging spectacularly towards the shallows of the lee shore. We had seconds to react. Within a minute the engine was running and we weighed the anchor and picked up a mooring after several aborted attempts. The wind was rising considerably and the gusts were sufficiently violent as to be able to stop Drumlin dead in her tracks as we were taking way off to pick up the mooring buoy making the whole exercise rather more difficult than is usual by any standards. I was doubly unimpressed by the need to shell out money to pay to park!

(Pasta and Sausages)

Scotland

Scenic are the mountains high,
Cold and damp, so rarely dry,
Overcast with cloud, the sky
Threatens rain; the sun so shy!
Long her days in summer's cool,
Always dark a lochan's pool,
Never short the winter's rule,
Divine creation, God's fair jewel.

Andrew Dalby, Arisaig, 18th May 2014

Tuesday 20th May 2014, Arisaig, N1-6 Sunny, Day 581:
How is it that XCWeather (an internet weather forecast site) and the Shipping forecast can be so different? It is like the old saying that a man with a clock knows the time, but a man with two clocks is never quite sure!

I took a walk up to StMary's Catholic Church for a look, but I could not see a way into it that did not involve going through the Minister's garden. In the graveyard, in an unmarked grave, lay the remains of Alistair M^{ac}Donald a poet who wrote in Gaelic and was the first to be published in that language in about 1751. This chimes with Samuel Johnson's comments on what he refers to as "Erse" culture which, as he observed, had until recently been an oral tradition of a nation that was, "Wholly illiterate". [37]

"... in those times nothing had been written
in the Erse language." [38]
Samuel Johnson

The following information is taken from material displayed on the notice board outside St Mary's Church in Arisaig which I noted down on my visit with amplifying information I have added from my own research.

The poet Alexander M^{ac}Donald (better known in Gaelic as Alasdair M^{ac}Mhaighstir Alasdair) b. circa 1698 at Dalilea in Moidart is buried in an unmarked plot somewhere in the graveyard of St Mary's church, Arisaig. He was the son of an Episcopalian [39] minister from the island Finnan and a descendant of the M^{ac}Donalds of clan Ranald. Educated at Glasgow University he became renowned for his widely acclaimed poetry on account of its powers of description, wit, daring, vigour, vitality and originality. Today he is considered one of Scotland's finest poets credited with bringing new vitality to traditional Gaelic verse.

The religious charity the Society in Scotland for the Propagation of Christian Knowledge SSPCK, formed in 1709 by Royal Charter (11 years after the original SPCK) employed him as a schoolmaster and catechist [40] from 1729 for 15 years. In the first 2 hundred years of its existence the society created numerous charitable schools for poor children aged between 7 – 11 years old. (Our modern idea of primary and secondary education arises from these institutions, and SPCK also trained people for the teaching profession). The purpose behind this work was to place schools:

"Where religion and virtue might be taught to young and old" in the Scottish Highlands and other "uncivilised" areas of the country, thus countering the threat of Roman Catholic missionaries achieving "a serious landslide to Rome" and growing Highland Jacobitism." [41]

Put simply it was an anti Catholic education program aimed at subduing a potentially hostile insurgency against an unloved Government. It was during this period that he is said to have written most of his poetry including his masterpieces Song of Summer (O'ran an t-Samhraidh) and The Sugar Brook (Allt an t-Siucair) inspired both by the landscape of the area and the fashionable English literature of the time. In 1741 Alexander MacDonald was also the first person to publish a non-religious book in Gaelic, an SSPCK school dictionary entitled "A Gaelic and English Vocabulary".

Over time Alasdair became increasingly disillusioned with the SSPCK which, inspired by the prospect of another second rising [42] under Prince Charles Stuart, lead him to write rousing political verse, some of which was sent abroad to exiled Jacobites to incite an armed expedition. When Charles finally arrived at Borrowdale on 25th July 1745 Alasdair was made a captain in the Clan Ranald Regiment as well as the Prince's Gaelic tutor.

Ultimately the coup ended once and for all in failure at the last battle to take place on British soil at Culloden near Inverness on 16th April 1746. Of the roughly equally numerical forces opposing each other, some 7-8000 on each side, a mere 50 Government troops were killed and 259 wounded contrasted with some 1500 – 2000 Jacobites killed. Subsequently reprisals took place in the Highlands under the Duke of Cumberland which had the intention of destroying the clan system and wiping out Gaelic culture. Like many others involved in the uprising Alasdair was forced into hiding and ultimately ended up on the island of Canna as the factor, [43] but he remained throughout his life an enthusiastic believer in the cause he had fought for.

Alasdair's collection "Ais-eiridh na Sean Chànoin Albannaich (The Ressurection of the Ancient Scottish Language) printed in 1751 was the first book of Gaelic poetry ever published and opens with an impassioned plea for the value and power of the language of the Gael. Copies of Ais-eiridh were burnt by the public hangman in Edinburgh because it also contained seditious Jacobite songs! Eventually Alasdair ended up living near Arisaig where he finished his greatest work Birlinn Chlann Ragnhaill (The Galley of Clan Ranald) an epic poem describing a sea voyage from South Uist to Carrickfergus in County Antrim in Northern Ireland. His final poem Fàilte na Mór-thir praises the lands of the clan Ranald where he spent most of his life, and where he died in 1770.

(Ratatouille, pasta and new potatoes)Free Night 190/49

Weather!

Rain, rain. What a pain!
Wind, wind. What a sin!
Cloud, cloud. What a shroud!
Weather, weather. Oh whatever!

Andrew Dalby, Arisaig, 21st May 2014

Carpe Diem

The dread of dying before I'm done,
That's my greatest fear.
Much to do, so much time gone,
Not yet been what I held dear.
Why were the dreams, born in my youth,
Cast off and laid aside?
What reason did I have to think
On earth I'd long reside?
And now I want to bear them up,
To run, to make them rise,
As older, weaker, frailer, I
Progress t'ward my demise.

Hold fast your goals, don't let them go,
Stay faithful to your cause.
Live out your dreams, help them to grow,
And never stop, or pause.
Study hard and show yourself
A workman who's not ashamed [44]
To strive to live the life you want,
Use best what time remains.
Carpe diem, seize the day! [45]
Don't put your dreams on hold.
Make the most of rest and play - and,
Have no regrets when you grow old.

Andrew Dalby, Arisaig, 23rd May 2014

Sunset

Below the rim of earth's west view,
The sun bows out of sight,
And radiates a smile of rouge,
Which ushers in the night.

Awash the sky emblazoned red,
A ruby swathe of light
Silhouettes the mountain heads,
And ushers in the night.

The evening air is cool and calm,
Yet hot celestial embers bright
Pierce the gloom with sunset's charm,
To usher in the night.

Andrew Dalby, Arisaig 24th May 2014

Sunday 25th May 2014, Arisaig, NE2-3 Broken Cloud, Day 586:
I went ashore twice today for water and to walk the dogs. We have otherwise spent the day quietly reading. The weather seems at last to be offering an opportunity to venture northwards, so after a trip ashore tomorrow for provisions we may head for Isle Ornsay on Skye.

(Vegetable Curry)   *Free Night 195/54*

Monday 26th May 2014, Isle Ornsay Harbour, Skye, Var 1 or less Rain Showers, Day 587:
We left Arisaig at about 10.30 am local time after I had been ashore for a few groceries. No sooner had we weighed the anchor and the rain arrived! The wind, such as it was,

was negligible and variable so we motored for 6 hours to get here.

Ornsay is a pretty little place and we will go ashore hopefully tomorrow to explore the area which appears to be a scattered settlement rather than obviously a village. The bay is also shallow and we may be able to dry Drumlin out for a peak at her anode and hull.

There is no telephone or 3G signal although BT Open Zone would like to charge me £4 for an hour of internet. No thank you!

Malaig smelt of fish, Armadale hid and there was a big modern building north of it which is the Gaelic College and Archive. There was a ruined castle at Knock Bay.

The ruined 15th century Knock Castle [46] lies approximately 5 miles north or Armadale on the east side of the Isle of Skye overlooking the Sound of Sleat. Known in Gaelic as Caisteal Chamuis (Castle Camus) it was once a stronghold of the clan M[ac]Donald. Originally built by the M[ac]Leods the castle changed hands between them and the M[ac]Donalds several times in its history and was finally abandoned in 1689.

Here at the head of the little loch of Isle Ornsay is an hotel circa 1750 and we are wondering if it is an English Army structure from after the Jacobite rebellion? Also what is the cube shaped building on the shore? A smokehouse or mill wheel?

(Sausages, Eggs and Beans)   *Free Night 196/55*

Tuesday 27th May 2014, Isle Ornsay Skye, Sunny – Heavy Rain in Evening, Day 588:

An hour and a half before low tide (1230) we kedged Drumlin into the shallows to dry her out! We didn't think we would succeed in seeing the anode, but we were happy to practise the theory knowing we'd get enough rise of tide to float us off. Another time we shall do it at high tide to properly dry her off.

We also cleaned some of the gelcoat and took up the saloon floor and removed the bilge water and cleaned the carpet.

(Bolognaise / Pasta)   *Free Night 197/56*

I wrote the following thoughts today on my mobile phone.

In economics there is a presumption that growth is both good and necessary. So it is in the arts which seem to value novelty and innovation. To some degree, and in certain circumstances, these qualities may be desirable, but they are not always necessary. Why grow beyond what is necessary or even sustainable? Therein lays excess and even greed. This is the foolish doctrine being preached by the financial institutions and political classes which is causing so much global inequality and unsustainable exploitation of the planet's resources, and which is driving the world on an ever accelerating

74

path to certain economic, social and environmental disaster. The great economist E F Schumacher cautioned against unlimited growth decades ago and so far his warnings have not been generally heeded. [47]

In the arts novelty does not have to mean reinventing or continually pushing boundaries, it can be achieved through variety. Innovation and progress, whilst sometimes useful in the arts, are not necessarily what should define a work as good or worthy. A work of art is good and worthy if it achieves its purpose whatever that is, just as a stable business making a profit but not greedily chasing wealth, growth and expansion is a good thing. How often do we see businesses expand too quickly and implode or get taken over by a bigger rival? So, whilst a growth in business can be good, it is not the only end to pursue or sole measure of success. So, in the arts great works can happen in the realm of the status quo as well as in the new and progressive. After all, most of us live in conventional houses, which may differ widely in style and value, and only a few live in

unconventional   architecturally
innovative structures.

    Some will say for economics to work
there needs to be, like in electrical
circuits, a potential difference. This is a
spurious justification for unjustifiable
inequality. My stomach feels hunger,
there is the motivation to seek food, my
home is cold, the need for fuel, thus the
potential to trade exists without making
some more rich than others. We share
and distribute as need wanders just as
nomads follow the herds.

CHAPTER FIVE

Over the Sea to Skye

"Follow the money" [48]

Wednesday 28th May 2014, Isle Ornsay Skye, Fair NE2-3, Day 589:

We dried out today properly and had a good look at Drumlin's anode, which is in good condition. The antifouling seems to be in better condition than expected too. One lesson learned though – DO NOT GO UNDER THE HULL! Drumlin quite swiftly, and without any warning, gracefully sank her starboard keel into the sand right up to the chines. Had anyone been underneath her at the time they could have been trapped, crushed or drowned. Or all three!

A couple of hours later as the tide rose she floated off perfectly well. We, as it turned out correctly, decided to bleed the stern tube, it was necessary even after such a short period out of the water. The stern tube is a close fitting rubber collar that goes around the propeller shaft and it stops water leaking into the boat where the shaft goes through the hull. When dried out this rubber collar drains the water leaving an airlock. The water is required to keep the rubber cool and stop it from melting by the heat generated by friction as the propeller shaft rotates when motoring.

Today we also heard the familiar "chuff chuff" sound of a steam engine that we have become accustomed to, only to realise we were hearing it in the wrong place. During our stopover in Arisaig we saw The Jacobite Steam Train coming through the station every day from Fort William to Mallaig and back. (Arisaig is mainland Britain's most westerly railway station). [49] *Today we were a long way from a railway line; the oh-so familiar sound was our old friend Waverley. We had not expected to see her out here. She was heading north towards Kyle Rhea.*

Another achievement of the day was a walk ashore with the dogs. This is a lovely little village with all the essentials, hotel, phone box, art gallery, tweed shop with ice creams, and a Gaelic whisky merchant. All of life's little necessities! This time last year we were on Gigha having escaped from Port Ellen on Islay where we had been pinned down by gales and I was having real problems with the islands amenities, or *rather lack of them! (See Monday 14th April 2014 page 53) Things have improved since then I am pleased to say!*

(Yorkshire Pudding, Soya Chunks and Vegetables in Sauce)

Free Night 198/57

Thursday 29th May 2014, Kyleakin Skye, Warm Overcast Var/NW3, Day 590:

The weather has been warm and muggy today with little or no wind until we reached Loch Alsh where it blew up to a fresh north westerly. We departed Isle Ornsay at about 13.00hrs in order to catch the north going tide through Kyle Rhea, the narrows that separate the Isle of Skye from the mainland. We had to use the engine! Today is a spring tide and as we chugged along at 3.8 knots into the narrows our progress quickened due to the resulting venturi effect and the reading on the log rose to 8.9 knots. Swift as this may sound the 5 or so knot increase was somewhat shy of the 8 knots we had been lead to believe is normal by the pilot books. Never-the–less, had we changed our minds and turned around we could not have escaped!

The ferry from Kyle Rhea to Glenelg crosses the narrows at its south entrance and is plying her trade in some seriously colourful waters with whirlpools, eddies and overfalls making the surface look decidedly confused and textured. As we swept through we were surrounded by seals casually patrolling the tucks and folds of the multiple layers of water, nonchalantly satisfying their curiosity about us as we wafted through their play and feeding ground, whilst their young cubs basked on the rocks by the water's edge.

Once through the narrows and into clear water in Loch Alsh we hauled the dinghy aboard, deployed our fenders and readied our warps to go alongside in the Kyleakin marina. We were met on our arrival by Claire's parents Jean and Richard and her sister Bridget; a lovely surprise as they'd come to greet us and to celebrate my 52nd birthday. We adjourned to the "Saucy Mary" restaurant for a birthday meal. As we came out after our meal we were treated to a "fly past" by the Waverly as she careered at full speed under the Skye Bridge towards Loch Alsh where a pipe band was on parade to welcome her. It has been a good day to be 52!

Kyleakin, and I am almost too embarrassed to mention him AGAIN, is a corruption of Kyle Haakon. Yes him, that old Viking of 1263. Saucy Mary is also a historical Viking figure.

Overlooking Kyleakin harbour is the ruined Castle Moil, [50] a 15th century ruined fort. There is a local legend associated with this site that predates the present structure which claims a Norwegian princess kept watch holding a chain across the loch to the mainland and charging tolls to passing boats; her name was Saucy Mary. Beinn na Caillich, which is Gaelic for "mountain of the old woman", is the large mountain behind the castle ruins where it is said she is buried.

I forgot to mention that we were impressed by a fisherman. Now there's a first! In Isle Ornsay there is an open boat about 20 feet in length and every morning at about 9am a young man, probably between 19 and 25 years old, takes it to sea potting for crustaceans! It is a hard and lonely life and this young man seems quite unafraid of hard work. His boat is called Fulmar.

Just after we moored up and Jean, Richard and Bridget were saying hello we saw an otter running along the path at the top of the pier, bold as brass, and ironically right past the front of the Eilan Ban Trust Bright Water Visitor Centre! We may go in and "Tarka" look at it...

Friday 30th May 2014, Kyleakin, Sunny, Day 591:
After breakfast we walked with the dogs over the Skye Bridge to Kyle of Loch Alsh to do the shopping. From the bridge we saw an otter by Gavin Maxwell's house on the

island. Very fitting. An expensive shop in the supermarket done, we returned by bus to Drumlin. The driver, a nice chap, was a painter and decorator by trade who had lived in Nottingham, came from Glasgow but had married a Skye girl; so he moved here. He admitted that though the scenery is beautiful he was now unmoved by it and it was normal. I think he found bus driving a boring job!

The locals are friendly. Davy, a young plumber, owns a Trapper yacht and was very chatty, as was an Irish gentleman the skipper of Zeus which swings on a private mooring in front of Saucy Mary's restaurant out in the Kyle.

This evening I saw a yacht coming towards the pontoon and Claire and I warped Drumlin along moving her closer towards a neighbouring fishing boat to make more room for "L'eau Life" to come alongside. We assisted with her lines. Her crew were rushing to make warps ready and were "a bit behind the curve". We all brought her in safely. Her skipper was a lovely gentleman by the name of, if my memory serves me correctly, Mr Mahmoon. Claire insists it is Mr Mahood. Our apologies to the gentleman for not accurately recording this. *He claimed that his name comes from his unusual ancestry which stems from a whole Irish clan who's origin is Iraqi. Apparently they were originally middle eastern refugees skilled in the weaving trade who had migrated to France, but were further dislocated along with the Huguenots when they fled the 18th century French religious persecutions. Ultimately settling in Ireland they brought with them the cultivation of flax and contributed to the birth and rise of the textile industry. Mr Mahmoon was one of those rare and gifted men with whom conversation was not only stimulating and interesting, but also full of wit and good humour which at times was outright funny too. We also had an acquaintance in*

common in the form of Billy the harbourmaster at Glenarm –
A man we both hold in high esteem.

(Stew and Dumplings)

Sunday 1st June 2014, Plockton, Variable 2 Overcast and
Cool, Day 593:
*I went ashore for a wander today. This is a lovely village. I
found the information boards which tell of Plockton's
naissance as a fishing village in the 1800s as the surrounding
estate was cleared for sheep! After the herring boom slumped
the potato famine hit making this place known as "The Poor
Village".*

*Yesterday we saw lots of old dinghies racing in the bay.
These boats are the heritage of 1933's regatta which was an
attempt to revitalise and save the local sailing skills which*

were in danger of being lost. Having watched the local youngsters sail there is no evidence of loss of skill and intuition for the art of sailing!

(Oaty Bake)   *Free night 200/59*

The village of Plockton came about as a result of the clearances [51] and what we today see as a cute Scottish hamlet nestled in the magnificent surroundings of the Scottish Highlands essentially began at best as a social experiment, or at worst a refugee camp depending on your point of view. One tends to imagine that these places have existed for many centuries, but sometimes the realities are quite different. Some of these apparently antique gems turn out to be little more than imitations, pastiches, fakes!

Plockton began in the early 1800s as the place where, to improve the value of his estate, landowner Sir Hugh Innes dumped his tenants when he cleared his land to make room for more profitable sheep, forcing farmers to turn to the sea as herring fishermen. At the time it was not unusual to have 2 families residing in each of the sea front crofts trying to eke out a living from growing food in the small strips of land behind their houses or from the sea. Imagine the overcrowding and poverty this would have lead to! By 1846 disaster overtook Scotland as the herring stocks plummeted and the potato famine took hold. Much of the village's history is proudly displayed on information boards near the car park and it makes me a little angry to say the least when I read the following quotation when set against this historic background of the time:

" The village is an Outstanding Conservation Area, which
ensures its character is preserved by building
guidelines and allows future generations

> to appreciate its unique and
> historic setting."

I cannot imagine that in 150 years time that we would be so blind as to the truths of history that we will seek to beautify and sanitise 20th and 21st century sites of human misery such as wartime internment camps, or the refugee camps at Sangatte, Calais, Algeria, Mauritania etc whether they be temporary of more permanent. The fact is that what we now blindly enjoy on a dreamy nice day out began with the nightmare of human suffering, and the custodians of these places seek to divert or distract the casual visitor from facing the uncomfortable and unacceptable truths of history so that we can "appreciate its historic setting"! If we are to really appreciate anything it should be that what happened to the indigenous Scottish people continues to happen today to even more vulnerable peoples such as the Kawahiva tribe of the Amazon, The Guarani Indians of Brazil, the Bushmen in Botswana, the Bayaka in the Republic of Congo, the Baka "Pygmies" and their neighbours in Cameroon and the list goes on; all are the victims of persecution and genocide at the hands of various organisations from big businesses to conservation organisations aided actively or tacitly by national governments. [52] Nevertheless, Plockton is a beautiful place in a stunning part of the world and its current residents enjoy a better way of life than their ancestors presumably did.

Thursday 5th June 2014, Churchton Bay Raasay, N2 Overcast and Rain, Day 597:
We left Plockton in fine drizzle and still air bound for the island of Raasay between the east side of Skye and the mainland. So much for the Met Office's promise of N or NE 4-5; however, we did manage to sail from just east of the Crowlins to the starboard hand marker buoy NE of Scalpay. This is another Boswell and Johnson venue.

"The Approach to Rasay [*sic*] was very pleasing. We saw
before us a beautiful bay, well defined by a rocky
coast; a good family mansion; a fine verdure
about it, with a considerable number of
trees; and beyond it hills and
mountains in gradation
of wildness." [53]
James Boswell

*Considering the time of year it is cold, even for this
latitude. On the plus side I finished reading the "Concise
Oxford History of Music" today, cover to cover! I am now
bereft of stimulating reading material!*

"Near the house, at Raasay, is a chapel unroofed
and ruinous, which has long been used
only as a place of burial." [54]
Samuel Johnson

Friday 6th June 2014, Churchton Bay Raasay, Warm and Broken Cloud, Day 598:

We took the dogs ashore this morning and explored the harbour and gun battery. We also met Paul, a regular holidaymaker here from Arnside in the Lake District. He kindly gave us a map of the island and told us about its attractions. Like us he is a dog owner and has a couple of Labradors, but not only was this a point of common interest, he also told us about the house he is doing up in Arnside which is very close to Willow Dene the guest house where Claire's parents regularly stay on holiday in Arnside! Small world...

In the afternoon we went ashore again to find the village, the shop and the remains of an ancient broch. After a not too long walk we arrived in Inverarish and soon located the shop which is also the post office. I went in and bought some provisions.

The shop had been recently refurbished and has just come into local community ownership. Speaking with the proprietor I learned that he is from Glasgow but married to a local lady and we reminisced about the penny trays and ice-cream vans of our youth and how as a consequence of the stifling effects of health and safety he was prevented from selling loose sweets or even from cutting ham and cheese on the premises without having to jump through endless hoops of red tape in order to comply with regulations. The result of all of this is that everything he sells has to be pre-packed! Despite these bureaucratically imposed shackles he runs a well stocked store. Prices are understandably higher than in the big supermarkets, but that is reasonably to be expected. I told him about my experience with Gigha this year and last, and I told him how impressed I was that Raasay community was remaining to some degree self-reliant despite an excellent ferry service to Sconser on Skye. He said that it is common amongst the locals to stock up with provisions for a week or more just in case the ferry cannot run or if the power supply fails. He also admitted that the ferry's regularity and reliability threatened the shop's existence as islanders can go to Portree on Skye or further for big shopping trips. This is another example of the unintended consequences of good intensions by government providing such a comprehensive ferry service!

Meanwhile, outside Bracken's howling brought a local lady out of her house offering to run Claire and the dog to the vet for treatment! That is how bad his caterwauling gets. The lady, perhaps in her forties, whose name was Jane volunteered that she had been a resident for about 9 years and that she has 2 old black dogs and a young Jack Russell. She thanked Claire for coming to Raasay! Really the privilege is ours for being able to visit and to be made so welcome.

We continued round the village and Claire and I parted ways, Claire to return home with the dogs and I to go into Borrowdale Wood in search of the broch. I found it on top of a steep hill where the forestry trees had been recently cleared. As ruins go it is quite unremarkable when one considers what it once was. It seems that the walls were robbed out to make the foundations for the school in the early 1700s.

(Tuna Pasta)   *Free Night 205/64*

Saturday 7th June 2014, Gedintailor Skye, Sunny Heavy Rain in Evening, Day 599:

The forecast was for the northerly/easterly tendency of the wind to come round to the south so we decided to cross the Narrows of Raasay to shelter in the bay at Gledintailor called Camas a Mhor-bheoil. Happily we sailed most of the way; all 1 mile of it, but anchor weighing and setting requires some use of the engine so we clocked up another 35 minutes! The morning and afternoon were gloriously sunny, but as 6pm loomed the clouds began to form and the wind whipped up from the west giving us a couple of hours closely monitoring our transits whilst our stern swung seductively, like a flamenco dancer's rump, at the rocky lee shore. Eventually the wind dropped and so did the rain; from a great height.

Frustratingly we were only a mile away from our last anchorage which had full 3G and phone signal, here we have intermittent phone and fleeting flickers of internet!

I tried an experiment today. Boiled sweets. Take 2 spoons full of sugar, 1 of honey and heat in a pan until it melts. Do not let it boil. Drip the molten confection into a bowl of cold water, strain quickly and dry. The result resembled the scraps of batter one finds in the bottom of the newspaper after eating fish and chips, but tasted like a cross between honey and toffee. I will try again sometime perhaps using lemon or fruit juice. Interestingly the sound of the mixture cooling in the water was like a blacksmith quenching wrought iron, so be careful, it is hot!

(Hot Chili, Veg and Rice.)   *Free Night 206/65*

Monday 9th June 2014, Rona, Variable 2-3 Sunny, Day 601:

I rowed ashore today and went for a walk.

89

I had read about the Church Cave in Haswell-Smith [55] that had been the islanders' place of worship until 1912 when a church was built. He states that it is still the tradition on the island to baptise babies there and that the last service to be held there was in 1970 led by the Very Reverend Dr James Matheson.

I soon found the detour to the cave church so I went for a look. Caves unnerve me as do mines and tunnels. I am conscious of the colossal weight of rock and earth bearing down from above, and of my own fragility and vulnerability beneath such magnitude. I was brought to thinking about "The Rock" on which the Church is built and the irony of this church being in, or under, rather than on a rock. I was also mindful of the burden of guilt and overbearing atrocities the Church has inflicted on people through its teachings and dogmas throughout history, and of the perversions and lies it has pedalled in the name of a God who would not recognise His own words when spoken by many fanatical Christian preachers. The hardship and austerity many people were subjected to, and still are, by zealots of any religion is something I come across time and time again when reading history, visiting historic sites, or for that matter listening to the news. The result is that I have written another anti-church poem. If anything annoys me it is the practices of religion that makes following a spiritual path an austere hardship of joyless penance. IT SHOULD NOT BE! Admittedly 80% of the 10 commandments [56] are negatives, thou shalt nots, 30% of them concern God and 50% relate to our behaviour towards others. The 2 positive commandments concern positive treatment of holidays (holy days) and the elderly. Personally I like the Wiccan Rede, it is clear and concise: If it harms none, do what you will. Don't take this at face value, think about it! This is probably the hardest rule to live by if you really try to observe it.

(Tomato and Lentil Soup with Dumplings and Salad) Free Night 208/67

These are the rocks

There is a church within a cave
Where people used to meet,
So dark and dank this hole-y nave,
Boulders for pews and stones for seats.

They'd trudge o'er miles of heath and heather,
And risking life and limbs
Wade through the bogs, defying weather,
To sing their sacred hymns.

The preacher stood (light to his rear!)
His congregation cornered,
And spoke his sermon, "The deaf shall hear!"
And thus their God was honoured?

Inside that cleft [57] those pious people
Beheld the parson's silhouette.
Undermined, that mountain's steeple...
The prayers they offered still echo yet.

Beneath "this rock I will build my Church" [58]
At the mouth of the gates of Hell,
And there in the damp their souls they did search,
And said, "He hath done all things well". [59]

So in that dungeon, their spiritual home,
They were burdened with sin and guilt,
All under the weight of tonnes of stone;
These are the rocks on which The Church is built!

Andrew Dalby Rona 9th June 2014

On Tuesday 10th June 2014 in Rona I wrote the following on my mobile phone:

> I've been thinking a lot since embarking upon this seafaring nomadic life style about landing fees, mooring fees and other such charges exacted by people who "control", for want of a better word, places best suited to the access of land by mariners. I want to pose a question:

Is it morally acceptable to charge
someone to set foot on land?

The Crown Estate in the United Kingdom is the body
responsible for the seabed. One would hope and expect it to
be a fair and unbiased official body:

"We are a commercial organisation with responsibility to
manage assets sustainably, working hand-in-hand
with Scotland's organisations, agencies and
individuals, for the benefit of local
businesses and communities." [60]

It in effect owns the sea bed and is the body to which
application has to be made if you want to establish a mooring,
a fish farm or other permanent or floating fixture. [61] It is
subject to rules similar to planning applications for buildings
and so forth, and they can levy a fee in the form of a type of
ground rent. This excludes temporary anchoring in the UK,
although other countries are known to charge for that too. The
important point here is that the Crown Estate is "a commercial
organisation" whose remit is concerned with facilitating the
making of money "for the benefit of local businesses". Further
to this, private entities who control access points to the shore
can, and often do, exact dues from sailors for landing. They
often monopolize the whole of an area or the only practical
points of access thereby leaving the person coming ashore
with little or no choice but to pay. On top of this, I feel that
fees are often disproportionately high in relation to the
services or facilities provided. In support of these provisions
one can argue that the infrastructure has to be provided and
maintained and that they serve the local economy. This is true,

and where it benefits communities is to be supported, but only when those benefits are gained ethically.

Anyone sailing these waters for any length of time will become aware of the proliferation of moorings encroaching into traditional anchorages leaving little room if any at all for a vessel to put down chain and lay secure. Where facilities are provided that enable mooring where naturally it would not have been possible, a legitimate service has been supplied, and it is reasonable as a visiting mariner to recompense the provider with gratitude. In such circumstances I can echo the words of Henry David Thoreau:

> "I have never declined paying the highway
> tax, because I am as desirous of being
> a good neighbor [*Sic*] as I am
> of being a bad subject." [62]
> Henry David Thoreau

A counterargument can be made that the sea is not like land which is owned, separated and divided by boundaries. It is freely accessible, not generally able to be portioned out to individual interests to the exclusion of others and is therefore not a legitimate resource for exclusive or segregated commercial exploitation, except for those mariners engaged in commercial activity. I am not entering here into international aspects of exclusion, just those at a purely human level within the community and within the nation. I would also assert that exclusive rights to those parts of the sea shore particularly situated such that they enable the easiest and safest access to and from the land should NOT be used as a source of personal or corporate gain or a business, and at most (if specialist engineering or equipment is provided to render a place effective as such, a landing where it otherwise would be difficult or impossible) that it be entirely charitable and not for profit where the leisure, none commercial activities of the general public are concerned. Many times places naturally suited for use as landings are "requisitioned" through the processes of application to the Crown Estate for commercial purposes and traditional anchorages can be swamped with moorings rendering them unsuitable for anchoring thereby securing a monopoly for those charging fees whilst effectively removing the opportunity for anchoring.

The argument that the Crown or any owner of property has legal right or rights to exploit their assets and to make charges of persons coming ashore is correct. These rights exist and there are laws to protect them, but this is not enough to answer the original question. Is it morally acceptable to charge someone to set foot on land? The issue is not one of legitimacy but of morality. It is not enough to be able to say I can do this because I can get away with it!

> "Unjust laws exist; shall we be
> content to obey them..." [63]
> Henry David Thoreau

I believe that any insistence, rule or law that requires a person seeking access to land from water, to pay is immoral for reasons I shall explain. It was Jean-Jacques Rousseau who in my view correctly defined natural law in his "A Discourse on Inequality":

> "... j'y crois apercevoir deux principes antérieurs à la
> raison, dont l'un nous intéresse ardemment à notre bien-être
> et à la conservation de nous-mêmes, et l'autre
> nous inspire une répugnance naturelle à
> voir périr ou souffrir tout être sensible
> et principalement nos semblables." [64]
> Jean-Jacques Rousseau

Roughly translated Rousseau says that he can see 2 principles at work; the first is an interest in our own wellbeing and self preservation; and the second an aversion to seeing another creature suffer, especially another human being. Put simply man is a land animal, the sea is an inherently hostile environment to him, and to seek to gain pecuniary advantage by breaking Rousseau's second natural law by denying, restricting or in any way imposing conditions on someone seeking terra firma is fundamentally wrong, immoral, unacceptable and above all contrary to natural law. It is against our natural instincts as humans, at least before they are corrupted by the vice of greed. So to those who administer these taxes upon the sailing community I urge them to heed the words of Henry David Thoreau,

> "... if it is of such a nature that it requires you to
> be the agent of injustice to another,
> I say, break the law." [65]
> Henry David Thoreau

-oOo-

We are quite excited about the prospect of becoming grandparents in November and our thoughts lately are often about children. I wrote this children's poem today.

Jilly the Jellyfish

Jilly is a jellyfish,
All squishy with no bones,
She really likes the hermit crabs,
In shells among the stones.

Harry is a hermit crab,
All crusty tough and strong,
He really likes the lampreys
So shiny, swift and long.

Lorna is a lamprey,
So elegant and sleek,
She really likes the mussels,
Who laze around all week.

Mikey is a mussel,
His shell is dark and blue,
He really likes the octopi,
Eight legs, not four, not two.

Octavia is an octopus,
With tentacles front and rear,
She really likes the jellyfish,
With bodies almost clear.

So what does this rhyme tell you?
What does it have to say?
It doesn't matter what you are,
You are special in your way.

Andrew Dalby, Rona, 12th June 2014

Friday 13th June 2014, Churchton Bay Raasay, SW3 Showers, Day 605:
We often have the VHF radio on when we are at anchor in order to hear the day's weather forecast, but sometimes we get even better entertainment, some of which would be hard to dream up if you were writing fiction. As no vessels or individuals can be identified from the following entry from our log book so I include it here purely for your amusement...

We heard a couple of yachts being contacted by Her Royal Highness's Royal Navy politely advising them that they were entering the live torpedo firing range that exists to the east of the island of Raasay island and the mainland in which a dived submarine was actually engaged in firing! The first one responded by calling Stornoway Coast Guard on channel 16 to ask if this was correct! He was then told that he should listen to his radio as it is good practice to monitor channel 16. The second yachtsman was asked if he was carrying charts for the area as they clearly show the prohibited area of the range! All that sea and the big boys want to practise shooting next to the children's play park!

We relocated from Rona to Churchton Bay. Initially we tacked into the southerly and made it as far as Portree, but had to admit defeat from there onwards. We had managed about 40% of the trip into wind under sail.

Rona was one of those places where we were completely out of range of phone signal and it is good to have some signal now we are back in Churchton Bay and to be able to keep in touch with folks. We are hoping that our friends Norman, Elizabeth and Rachel may be able to meet up with us on Monday.

(Pasta, Soya and Mash)   *Free Night 212/71*

Saturday 14th June 2014, Day 606:
I wrote the following comments on my mobile phone:

> We have had an interesting time since leaving Kyleakin. First we went to Plockton where they filmed the television series *Hamish M[ac]Beth* which

starred Robert Carlyle. You know, the guy who played that baddie in that Bond film and got his kit off in The Full Monty!

The sailing club in Plockton has old dinghies from the 1930s. They are sailed regularly and are poetry in motion to watch. Like all dinghy sailors the locals are not shy about invading personal space, so visiting yachties need to make friends easily. The train line passes by too, so there is a lot going on. Happily it is not a through road so cars are not constantly zooming around.

After Plockton we went to Raasay, a beautiful island between Skye and the mainland with a thriving community. Continuing north took us to Rona where, in the days before the Union that is presently so much in the news, pirates hid preying on the weak and unwary on passage through these waters. We are now retracing our wake to Kyleakin for provisions and to meet up with friends. Then onwards to Gairloch and Ullapool.

Stay tuned!

Monday 16th June 2014, Kyleakin Harbour, N2 Sunny, Day 608:

We spent a very enjoyable day with our friends Norman, Elizabeth and Rachel. I was in Kyle of Lochalsh at the supermarket when they arrived, so Norman surprised me by coming over to help me back with the shopping. He just popped up from behind the tins when I wasn't looking!

Tuesday 17th June 2014, Churchton Bay (again), NW3 Sunny Periods, Day 609:

We left Kyleakin this morning and sailed into wind successfully covering about half the distance to Churchton Bay by tacking. We like it here and will wait until we have suitable wind to take us up to Gairloch.

I read a quotation from the Longitude Prize in an email I received from Amazon today saying, wait for it, that water (one of my favourite topics) is "a finite resource"! What a load of ... It is not as if water is like fossil fuels and part of the earth's capital assets. Perhaps what it should have said was FRESH water, but even then finite? Please! Anyone who has ever been to Wales or Scotland and has been caught in a shower knows that water is far from finite. The propaganda aimed at restricting, commercialising and promoting a "normalised" attitude towards water as being a commodity (which it is not) as something we must buy or pay for is an issue that makes me rather hot under the collar.

Many people will argue, and interestingly all those family and friends who have contended this point with me, are engineers by profession, that water needs a means of supply and distribution and that it needs purifying. Yes it does need purifying, to remove the noxious poisons and detritus with which modern industry and farming practices pollute the natural environment. The purification costs may vary depending on the quantity processed, but the infrastructure exists whether we use one litre or a hundred. I have yet to be persuaded by any argument to change my mind on this. EVERYONE HAS EQUAL RIGHT TO CLEAN DRINKING WATER WITHOUT COST. Furthermore, I object to being landed with the bill to pay for the purification of water because of the wonton disregard industry and business has towards polluting nature. This is a point of principle.

Wednesday 18th June 2014, Churchton Bay, NW3-4 Sunny, Day 610:

We went ashore this morning with the dogs. Claire went north and found [St]Moles Church just past the old stables and I went for bread and chopped tomatoes at the Inverarish village store. Whilst I was there I committed to my cause and bought shares in the Community of Raasay Retail Association Ltd. I am now a member of their co-operative! They seemed genuinely grateful for the support and for the vote of confidence. The shop was also bouncing again with customers and the post office part was open too. I think it is a form of crowd funding and the money invested goes into the business capital, you don't receive dividends, but I think you can withdraw your investment at face value if the business remains solvent. (Why would you?)

(Tuna Pasta)   *Free Night 217/76*

CHAPTER SIX

Through the Other End of the Telescope

"The Highland men and Island men
are ready for the fray." [66]

Thursday 19th June 2014, Badachro, Overcast, Day 611:
The Coast Guard Maritime Safety Information Broadcast
at 10.10 am today, and I quote, "Wind, north west 3 or 4." It
is not! It is northerly and hardly able to gust above 5 miles
per hour; that is force 2 maximum. Wrong on all counts. Why
does the British government invest so much in the
Meteorological Office? I will tell you why – Climate change
propaganda to serve their political ends and "green"
agendas which are far from environmentally friendly very
often! They might as well have an office for Tarot Cards and
Palm Reading.

After making the most of the paucity of wind we made it to
our destination. We tacked past Portree and gained a mile but
in truth motored most of the way to the north end of Rona. We
sailed across from there at about 2 knots. Interestingly as we
passed the Royal Navy Deep Sea Listening Post which is on
the north end of the island of Rona, the global positioning
system crashed, but only in the what would be the white sector
of a light house, which is very narrow. For heaven's sake; we
know you are there, it says so on the Admiralty charts. The
Russians probably know what is on the canteen menu, so why
go to the bother?

It has been a long time since we last came to Badachro; it
was our honeymoon in fact. We liked it then, and we still do.
We used to harbour a dream of running a little shop here.

They Can't See Me

There is a little sparrow
Sitting in the tree,
He can see the garden
But he can't see me!

There is a little squirrel
Climbing up the tree
She can see the sparrow,
But she can't see me!

There is a little rabbit
Running round the tree,
He can see the squirrel,
But he can't see me!

There is a little fish
In the pond beside the tree,
She can see the rabbit,
But she can't see me!

There is a little frog
By the pond beside the tree,
He can see the fish,
But he can't see me!

There is a little butterfly,
Flying past the tree,
She can see the frog,
But she can't see me!

There is a little hedgehog,
Underneath the tree,
He can see the butterfly,
But he can't see me!

All the little animals
Living by the tree,
They can see each other,
But they can't see me!

Andrew Dalby, Badachro 19th June 2014

When I wrote this poem I imagined it illustrated with a little child hiding behind a fence watching the garden on the left page and a Tree on the right. Each subsequent page would be the same as the one before but with another element added. Claire is a very gifted artist, but I have not been able to persuade her to illustrate this poem ... yet!

Friday 20th June 2014, Loch Shieldaig Gairloch, Overcast, Day 612:
This morning I rowed ashore and took a walk from Badachro village to Shieldaig Lodge Hotel. Unfortunately there is no internet or phone signal in most parts of this area, so I had to walk all the way to the hotel. Why? This is where Claire and I spent most of our honeymoon and when we were here we saw yachtsmen rowing from their boats to the lawn at the front of the hotel to come ashore for their evening meals. We thought this was really "cool" and frankly never imagined that we would ever be that type of customer. I went in and booked a table for two for tonight! On my return we had lunch and I told Claire what I'd done, so we weighed anchor and sailed the mile and a bit along the coast to Loch Shieldaig and anchored in front of the imposing and slightly

gothic facade of one of Scotland's last functioning Victorian hunting lodges. It is 5.30pm – Not long to dinner!

We have just returned from a lovely dinner of venison; it is just after midnight. Mr Lagerman, the proprietor we knew, had the lodge for 18 years, 13 years ago he sold it to Gino and Wendy Bernardi. We were the only guests for dinner in spite of the fact the hotel was fully booked for a wedding. Apparently all the wedding party were wining and dining elsewhere, so we were their sole focus of attention. Gino the proprietor is also a first rate chef and a fellow yachtsman so we were well entertained by him after we had eaten, and over coffee in the lounge we discussed yachting and sailing matters. Gino is in the process of selling the lodge and intends to cruise on his M^{ac}Wester 36. He showed us photographs of his beautifully appointed yacht. He has just sold his older and smaller yacht to a gentleman who comes to test his water

supply from the Highland Council; it turns out to be a colleague of Claire's brother. Small world!

Free Night 219/78

Saturday 21st June 2014, Loch Shieldaig, Overcast, Day 613:

After our late night we had a lay in this morning. I got up at about 10.30 and did some laundry, put the cockpit tent up and hung the clothes out to dry. I then decided to compose some music, so I assembled a note row, or series as they are sometimes called, and worked out its inversion, retrograde and retrograde inversion forms, but I did not transpose them. I wrote a study for trumpet from it. The piece needs refining and dynamics adding once I have decided upon the final form. I called the series the "Sheildaig Row". I plan to use it for a few pieces perhaps at a later date.

Naturally we did not feel like eating much today after our excesses yesterday.

(Homemade Pizza)   *Free Night 220/79*

Silence

It is the silence,
That velvet void,
The hollow darkness,
Where even ears cannot hear:

In the warm womb of nothing,
Where the loudest thing is a thought,
There is the reward of solitude,
The respite for a sage.

Be still and know... [67]

It is silence we should seek,
For questions find answers in quiet,
And wisdom is wrought
In the soundless serenity of our souls.

And after, that still small voice,
"What doest thou here..?
Go, return on thy way..." [68]

Andrew Dalby, Sheildaig Loch, 21st June 2014.

I have oftentimes been struck by the profound quiet of the silence in many of the anchorages we have stayed in and how my mind can continue to run rampant with chaotic thoughts and ideas all clamouring to be heard. We often look for rest on holidays, weekends or days off and allow our bodies time out, but do we allow our mind the same opportunity to calm down and repose? Sometimes to relax in silence is the only way to really hear anything. It is only in silence that we can truly listen, and only by listening that we properly hear. When did you last listen to yourself? When did you last hear that still small voice within?

"I like the silent church before the service
begins, better than any preaching." [69]
Ralph Waldo Emerson

Sunday 22nd June 2014, Loch Shieldaig, Cool Overcast and Rain, Day 614:
We stayed put in the loch today as it is sheltered here. A few local boats went racing this afternoon in the rain. I dug out my art equipment and sketched the ketch moored next to

us, after which I did a small watercolour of it. I should declare that I am to art what Joseph Mallord William Turner (1775-1851) was to computer programming. I have no talent whatsoever for it except in so far as the results of my effort rarely fail to cause mirth and hilarity in those that see it; especially me. There is a commonly held opinion that one cannot tickle oneself, well my own art work can tickle my funny bone to the point of reducing me to tears of laughter. As Claire always reminds me though, it is the process that is important. True, but the results are priceless.

(Soya Chunks and Mash)　　　　　　*Free Night 221/80*

Monday 23rd June 2014, Strath Bay Gairloch, Sunshine and Broken Cloud, Day 615:
We can now cross anchoring in Sheildaig Loch and rowing ashore to the lodge for lunch off our bucket list as we have now done what we witnessed there on our honeymoon 29 years ago. It was not something we ever really entertained any serious thoughts of achieving. It goes to show you what twists of fortune life can take. But it was time to move on, lovely as the loch is, there is no phone signal and we felt some contact with our offspring was called for.

Strath Bay is the wide open north east corner of Gairloch Loch and is basically the "seaside" of Gairloch village itself. The bottom is fairly shallow (3-4 metres) and consists largely of sand. It is a little prone to swell, but the winds are light so it is not uncomfortable.

Contact has been made with Hannah and Martin, I also checked in with my Dad: and Uncle Stewart has kindly retrieved our mail from Troon marina. We have also made arrangements with Claire's brother Nick for next weekend; they are coming over with the caravan, so we shall remain here. This is good as we have amenities here and we can delay going to Flowerdale Harbour for a top up of diesel. Nick has also kindly agreed to buy some more bulk provisions for us from the supermarket which will save us a lot of money sourcing goods locally.

Last year in Ardfern (Wednesday 5th June 2013) [70] we saw a man walking on water, today a man swam alone and apparently unsupported from the slip at Strath to the beach in front of the golf course at Gairloch Hotel. It took him about an hour. He was wearing a wet (or dry) suit so we imagine it was not his first time, and that he was properly catered for in his endeavour. He needed to be as the sea around here is alive with jellyfish!

(Traditional Fry Up)   *Free Night 222/81*

Tuesday 24th June 2014, Loch Shieldaig, W1-2 Sunny, Day 616:
I finally fixed the outboard motor having discovered how to remove the carburettor jets I cleaned them in vinegar. It runs like a lawnmower now. Claire didn't like the swell in Strath Bay so we decided to come back to Shieldaig Loch and anchored near a catamaran. Nick and Linda are coming over for the weekend so we are going to stay in this area until next week. I shall fill up with diesel on Friday at Flowerdale then we can head for Loch Ewe and then Ullapool. I put some teak oil on the forward woodwork today.

(Fried Rice and Lorne Sausage)   *Free Night 223/82*

Aphorism

They say a man is measured by the number of friends he
has. Be careful how you define a friend. It may be more
accurate to say a man is defined by the number of
dependants he has. In the final analysis most
people we deal with want us for some
reason, work, trade or assistance of
some other sort which is to their
benefit. Weed those out and see
who really is your friend, that
person who likes you, wants
your company, but requires
nothing of you.

Andrew Dalby, Sheildaig Loch, 25th June 2014

"To say that a man is your Friend, means
commonly no more than this, that
he is not your enemy." [71]
Henry David Thoreau

Saturday 28th June 2014, Strath Bay Gairloch, NE4-5
Sunny, Day 620:
*We left Drumlin lying at anchor for quite a lot of the day
setting off ashore at about 10.30 am and returning at 21.20.
The tandem anchors held her well whilst we went with Nick
and Linda in their car all the way to Big Sand at the north end
of the loch to walk the dogs and then up to Rubha Reidh
Lighthouse. We then had coffee in the Melvaig Inn before
returning to the caravan site for a tea of fish and chips.*

*This morning we were serenaded by the local pipe band
which was apparently processing from Gairloch to
Flowerdale just down the coast to launch a newly built Skiff.*

I copied the following off a poster in the village:

Gairloch St Ayles Skiff Launch
Saturday 28th June 2014
10 a.m

Starting at the GALE Centre, Gairloch
The skiff will be pulled along to the slipway at the harbour
in a procession including the Coastguard, Gairloch Pipe
Band,
and pupils from Gairloch High School.

The Launch Ceremony
11 a.m.
Performed by Mrs Janet Bowen, Lord-Lieutenant of Ross
and Cromarty

followed by rowing from the pontoon at the harbour where
the skiff will be on display – there may be an opportunity
for a short trip in the boat.

Afterwards there will be a BBQ at the harbour

All welcome

The St Ayles skiffs are community-built wooden boats,
now being seen all around
The Scottish coastal communities, and also further afield
worldwide.
They are used for racing with 4 rowers and a cox, but also
for pleasure rowing,
and the Gairloch skiff is a resource for the whole
community.

Sunday 29th June 2014, Loch Kerry, Sunny NNE2, Day 621:

When we got up Claire made oaty bake for lunch whilst I went ashore to collect the provisions that Nick and Linda kindly bought for us at the supermarket for us in Dingwall. Nick saw me coming and was already waiting at the jetty to load up. Having ferried the goods back to Drumlin Claire had finished cooking our lunch and we took it back to Gairloch Caravan Park where we spent the rest of the day. We had a ride out with Nick and Linda in the car to the beach in front of Gairloch Hotel to walk the dogs and afterwards enjoyed an ice-cream in Flowerdale. Whilst we were there we saw the skiff that the community had built at the boat club. Claire and I also did a recce of the pier in advance of going in with Drumlin to take on fuel and water next week. We also saw the weather forecast posted in the harbour office window which promised gales on Wednesday, so we shall keep an eye on that situation before committing to sail round into Loch Ewe. We also managed to speak to Hannah who seems to be in good spirits at the moment with the early pregnancy sickness getting less and her general rotundity greater! As evening approached Nick and Linda made ready to tow the caravan home and once we had waved them off we returned home and motored back to the shelter and seclusion of Loch Kerry for the night.

(Oaty Bake)   *Free Night 228/87*

Tuesday 1st July 2014, Loch Kerry, N1-2 Sunny, Day 623:

It has been a beautiful day of sunshine. I cleaned off the algae growing on the rubbing strakes and Claire aired the bedding. We were intending to set off today but we would only have had to motor for 25 – 30 miles so we decided to ride out tomorrow's forecast of S/SW8-9 here in the relative shelter and security of Gairloch. Perhaps Thursday will be a suitable day with enough southerly to westerly wind to propel us safely to Loch Ewe. It is disappointing not to have any telephone signal here because I am concerned that Martin, Hannah and other family members will worry about us.

(Pizza)   *Free Night 230/89*

Wednesday 2nd July 2014, Loch Kerry, S-W8 Showers, Day 624:

The loch has been lively today with some swell caused by the wind, but generally it is good shelter in here in winds with little northerly component. I tried a bit more water colour painting again! I am still not very good at it, but I did do a charcoal drawing of a Canada goose that Claire though worthy of framing and hanging – if we had a wall. I suggested it might be worthy of the privy door.

It is 16.30 hrs and the weather has seemed to follow a classic warm to cold front passage and the wind shifts and visibility have conformed to type. If the bad weather doesn't kick off again I am right in my interpretation.

Well it is now 21.20 hrs, it is not raining and the weather is calm, there are however, dark clouds approaching, but so far the barometer is still steadily reading 1010mb. I wonder if this could be a new low coming rather than the back end of the last one as the winds are forecast to back and increase again force 5 – 8. Friday is set to be the same then the wind will veer northerly. Just what we need!

Other news – The reigning champion Andy Murray was knocked out of Wimbledon today in straight sets by Grigor Dimitrov.

(Yorkshire Pudding and Soya Mince) Free Night 231/90

Friday 4th July 2014, Loch Kerry, Rain then Fair Var8-1!, Day 626:
It occurred to me this morning that I have not mentioned how warm the wind has been since the sun left! This is probably because it has a large southerly component. It is pouring down at the moment (9.10 am) and although sheltered in here there are some very strong gusts of wind. They do not last long enough to put too much stress on the anchor and chain; we have 45 – 50 metres out.

Interestingly 4th July 1845 was the day that one of my heroes Henry David Thoreau moved into his "hut" on Walden Pond.

The 1 o'clock BBC News has just reported that Rolph Harris has been given 5 years and 9 months in prison for child abuse. He is 84 years old. He has been sentenced according to the tariffs for the time he committed the offences. Had he committed them since the mid 1980s he might have received any sentence up to life. It seems to me that in reality he has! Also the phone hacking trial gave "News of the World" editor Andy Coulson 18 months in prison and his companions about 6 months.

Claire made biscuits and I made tea, beyond that not much has happened today.

(Tuna Pasta)　　　　　　　　　　*Free Night 233/92*

Saturday 5th July 2014, Poolewe, SW2-4 Sunny, Day 627:

We sailed from Loch Kerry to the entrance of Loch Ewe, but had to motor against the wind to travel south down the loch. (We basically sailed in a "n" shape.) *It has been an interesting experience once again to view the familiar from an unfamiliar vantage point. Cove, Firemore beach and Inverasdale, our old favourite holiday haunts, seen for the first time from a retrospective position is a rare treat.*

There is a lot of history here, particularly relating to the two world wars and the second in particular. Loch Ewe is a deep water anchorage suited to large shipping and good use was made of it by the Royal Navy in the Second World War.

Osgood Hanbury Mackenzie, [72] son of the 12th Laird of Gairloch, built an estate near Poolewe on land acquired by his mother between 1862 and 1863. Initially he built a mansion house in the 1860s and afterwards turned the grounds into what is now the world famous Inverewe Gardens. He did not actually reside in the mansion all of the year, using it instead as a hunting lodge for paying guests engaged in shooting and fishing sport. In 1915 Osgood passed on the running of the estate to his Daughter and Son in law, Mairi and Robert Hanbury.

In the years before the First World War Loch Ewe was used by the Admiralty as it prepared for a potential conflict with Germany in the light of:

> "... her [Germany's] dream of a colonial empire,
> entailing her transformation from
> a land-power to a sea-power." [73]
> Erskine Childers

After the outbreak of war Loch Ewe was used as a secondary refuelling base for the fleet where ships could come to take coal aboard in the event that Scapa Flow was too dangerous for such activity due to a German submarine threat.

Robert Hanbury acted as a recruiting officer for the 4th Seaforth Highlanders and initially he found no shortage of young men willing to volunteer for active service. Local pride in the response to the call to arms was, like in many other areas of Britain, great, but before too long the awful truth of what this would mean in human terms was to dawn. On a more positive note he and Mairi were very cognisant of the needs of local people especially concerning the availability of food and were not miserly in their sharing of resources to those in most need. The estate was also a great resource of fresh food for naval vessels visiting the loch.

At the beginning of the Second World War the size of the German Bomber threat to the Royal Navy's fleet at Scapa Flow was overestimated, but in response to this perceived menace Loch Ewe [74] was chosen for its strategic position, and safe anchorage. Unfortunately, though less vulnerable from the air, it was more exposed to submarine attack. Ultimately Port A, as Loch Ewe was designated until March 1940, would serve only as a reserve base to Scapa Flow, but took on an important role as a transit anchorage and refuelling base for the Arctic convoys. As a consequence of this the whole area would become a restricted area and required local people to have special passes to move around.

In order to defend the Loch a number of systems were put in place including a guard loop (a magnetic sensor device) for detecting ship movements through the entrance to the Loch, a pair of 6 inch Naval Guns on the western shore, anti-submarine nets across the loch and a number of anti-aircraft guns. The defences headquarters were established and run from Tournaig House, once the home of Osgood Hanbury Mackenzie, his daughter Mairi and her husband Robert Hanbury who had played such an important role locally during the First World War.

By the end of 1941 concern was growing about the poor quality of officer material because such a high proportion of those put forward for commissions were being rejected by the Selection Boards; this lead to the establishment in 1943 of The Highland Fieldcraft Training Centre at Poolewe under the direction of Lord Rowallan. As a result of this training, many of Rowallan's graduates went on to distinguished service and many gave their lives for the cause of freedom.

Firemore beach has been a favourite holiday destination for our family for decades, indeed Claire and her family have been coming here since she was a small child and we in our turn brought our family here. Claire's brother Nick has continued the tradition most recently and has lobbied the Highland Council to maintain the access to the common land for campers and caravaners. Health and Safety being the blunt instrument it is, and with the ever present threat of litigation, there are those in authority who want to put an end to this ancient right of access on the grounds that there are insufficient "facilities" for water and waste disposal. The truth is that responsible campers provide their own sanitation and dispose of their waste responsibly, but a few have abused this to the detriment of the majority which has resulted in an emerging possibility of closure.

I heard the great news that my Godson Timothy Clark has graduated from university with a good honours degree. Well done Tim, we are all very proud of you.

Claire's brother Nick and sister-in-law Linda are in Leeds for the Grand Depart of the Tour de France! How the hell can trading standards allow this? If it is the tour of France, as the name implies, what is it doing in Blighty? Surely that fact alone makes it the Tour d'England! In 1993 [75] European Legislation came into force which protects food names on a geographical or traditional recipe basis. *The EU complains if you call it Kendal Mintcake if it isn't from Kendal or feta cheese if it isn't from Greece. I assume that the Tour de France comes under the same type of legal exemption for geographical accuracy as perhaps Mars Bars!*

One really positive thing about Poolewe is that we have a phone signal. This is good as we have been able to communicate with Martin and Hannah as well as the rest of the family. It is good to know that they are safe and well.

(Mash/Chile beans)   *Free Night 234/93*

Sunday 6th July 2014, Poolewe, S2-4 Sunny Scattered Showers, day 628:
The genoa has had some stitching deteriorating and the wind the other day didn't help, so today we took it down and did a lot of sewing. There is a little left to do still.

I walked the dogs ashore on the beach and road; they picked up a load of ticks. Yuk! Bracken fell out of the dinghy and we were shadowed ashore (and back to the boat) by a very curious and inquisitive seal. He/she came quite close to us all the way to the shore, perhaps within 5 or 6 feet. It also watched us as we walked along the road. The dogs didn't actually see it until we were coming back down from the road towards the beach and all the way back to Drumlin they were alert and watchful, but not upset by its presence.

Novak Djokovic beat Roger Federa in tennis at Wimbledon and Lewis Hamilton won the British Grand Prix today!

(Vegetable Curry)　　　　　　　*Free Night 235/94*

Firemore

Our family's little open secret place,
Venue of many days and weeks of rest,
That common land, those dunes, the beach, that grace
The shores of Ewe, the loch upon the west.

A once remote forgotten field of grass,
Where soldier guards kept vigil o'er the fleet,
Imperilled now by council rules alas
As health and safety guidelines cannot meet.

For decades people camped upon this ground,
Drew unpolluted water from the spring,
And rested body, mind and soul, unbound
Their human spirit soared on eagle's wings. [76]

Oh Firemore, dear Firemore 'tis clear,
The powers that be your natural virtues fear!

Andrew Dalby, Poolewe, 6th July 2014

Tuesday 8th July 2014, Ullapool, N1-2 Sunny Spells, Day 630:

We decided to make for Ullapool today so as to be here for 10th July, Claire's Mum Jean's birthday. It will also be our second anniversary afloat. The wind was directly on the nose right up Loch Ewe, but we managed some sailing as we turned more eastwards. Amazingly, as we entered Loch

Broom, we not only had phone signal, but the internet returned too!

Yesterday evening and today were productive – I managed to write a long narrative poem about the shipwreck at cove in 1944.

(Pasta and Egg with Tuna and Onion Sauce)
Free Night 237/96

The Ballad of the William H Welch

Built in Bethlehem, one of the best that they made,
A Liberty ship for the tramping trade,
The William H Welch, March tenth forty three,
Blessed with more rivets, better fit for sea!
But the winds did blow and the waves did roar,
And the William H Welch for our liberty braved war.

At the launch of the first in her class, this prayer,
Pat Henry's great call to arms filled the air,
They said, "Give me liberty, or give me death!"
And what they had wished for was put to the test!
For the winds did blow and the waves did roar,
And the William H Welch for our liberty set forth.

The Vice Commodore ship, the second in line,
One gone before, another eight ships behind,
The convoy assembled, then bound for New York,
A perilous journey, but vital their work.
And the winds did blow and the waves did roar,
Still the William H Welch for our liberty set forth.

Dark and grim was that fateful night,
And Loch Ewe's safe haven was hid from sight,
A tiny small error, a slip at the helm,
And so she made way to the watery realm.
And the winds did blow and the waves did roar,
And the William H Welch lost her liberty; and more!

Soon she laid creaking and breaking apart,
And the storm that was raging would tear out her heart,
Ere long she was done for and could take no more,
On that February night nineteen forty four.
And the winds did blow and the waves did roar,
And the William H Welch was at liberty no more.

Captain Lee Marshall gave order to try
To seek out some refuge by climbing up high,
But one by one the crew fared not well,
As the sea washed them off with her monstrous swell.
And the winds did blow and the waves did roar,
And the William H Welch was at liberty no more.

By some great blessing and God's good grace,
Three men survived and came to a place,
The croft of M^{ac}Kenzie at the end of the road,
In a wee small hamlet by the name of Cove.
Still the winds blew and the waves did roar,
But the William H Welch was at liberty no more.

The alarm was raised and word was sent out,
And all that were able, the doughty, the stout,
Set forth to the site of that hellish mayhem,
To save whom they could of those helpless young men.
And the winds did blow and the waves did roar,
But the William H Welch was at liberty no more.

There they found by the rocks on the shore,
Men cold with exposure and chilled to the core,
Some naked, some dying, some dead on the beach,
And more in the waves just out of their reach.
And the winds did blow and the waves did roar,
But the William H Welch was at liberty no more.

Of the ship's compliment, all seventy four,
Only twelve lived who made it to shore!
So please do remember when hearing this story,
The sixty two dead "Promoted to Glory".
For the winds did blow and the waves did roar,
But the William H Welch has her liberty no more.

Andrew Dalby, Poolewe 7th July 2014

The SS William H Welch [77] was a liberty ship that was wrecked on the rocks at the entrance to Loch Ewe on the morning of Saturday 26th February 1944 during the Second World War. Although a British ship design they were made in America as a wartime expedient whose purpose was to be an easy to build, relatively cheap and "disposable" cargo ship; 2710 were constructed between 1941 and 1945 in 18 shipyards at a cost of about $2,000,000 each. They were made in sections and then assembled, the early ones being riveted together, but as the need increased for ever quicker and cheaper production, welding became the preferred method of construction. This change led to structural issues that caused cracking in the decks and hulls, sometimes with catastrophic results. Furthermore, Liberty Ships when empty were ballasted with water which could make them less stable and difficult to handle in certain conditions. They were not pretty ships either and had a poor public image, but on the day the first one was launched, the SS Patrick Henry, [78] President

Roosevelt reprised the words of a 1775 speech attributed to Patrick Henry himself:

"Is life so dear, or peace so sweet, as to be purchased
at the price of chains and slavery? Forbid it,
Almighty God! I know not what course
others may take; but as for me,
give me liberty, or give
me death!" [79]

It was as a result of this speech that the moniker Liberty Ship came about, and they were usually named after famous Americans. This particular Liberty Ship was named after William H Welch [80] (1850 – 1934) one of the Four main professors who founded the Johns Hopkins Hospital in Baltimore.

Wednesday 9th July 2014, Ullapool, N1-2 Sunny, Day 631:
I went ashore this morning and booked a table at the Seaforth restaurant for Jean's (Claire's mother) *birthday tomorrow, then I went to the Post Office and made myself known to the wife of my musician friend Stephen, who I worked with many moons ago. I later returned home armed with phone numbers and rang Stephen who kindly invited us up on Saturday evening for a curry.*

This afternoon Claire and I walked the dogs along the beach and discovered a couple "sunbathing"! Ahem... I returned Claire and the dogs home and then went in search of the supermarket and the book shop; both of which I found. On my way up the hill I was approached by a couple also seeking the supermarket and told them that I was on the same quest, so we walked together. They too were sailors in the process of circumnavigating the United Kingdom anticlockwise. I said we were going in the same direction around the Hebrides.

123

They had seen us at anchor though they admitted to having picked up a mooring. They went on to say that at £12 per night with no facilities provided, it is too expensive adding that the disclaimers often found on moorings warning that they may not be serviced or serviceable was an unacceptable state of affairs in their opinion. I quite agree with their sentiments. We also lamented the encroachment of moorings which seem to be everywhere taking over suitable anchorages. I think I have found kindred spirits in these matters.

The supermarket yielded good provisions and will no doubt be patronised by us again before we leave, as will the book shop which has a copy of the book on Loch Ewe's 2ⁿᵈ World War history that I need for my research.

On the Loch Broom Sailing Club slipway I met a lady and 3 children, 2 boys and a girl, fishing for crabs. They were there all afternoon. I helped retrieve a snagged fishing line for them from the dinghy. They caught lots of crabs, some quite large ones!

The rowers were out in force again and tonight 2 Toppers, an adult and child in each, entertained us with capsize drills to the obvious delight of the children judging by the sound of their giggling and laughter.

(Chili)   *Free Night 238/97*

Thursday 10ᵗʰ July 2014, Ullapool, Var <3 Sunshine, Day 632:
Today is the 2ⁿᵈ anniversary of our purchase of Drumlin.

We have had a quiet day in bright sunshine today. We walked the dogs then left them aboard whilst we went ashore to buy a birthday card and present for Claire's Mum Jean. Later this afternoon Jean, Richard and Claire's sister Bridget arrived and we joined them ashore. At 18.30 hrs Nick arrived with Linda, Charis and Matthew, and Margaret, Linda's mother and we all resorted to the Seaforth restaurant for a celebratory dinner.

There is a Scottish Coastal Rowing Association race meeting taking place this weekend and the crews have been gathering from far and wide today. When we were walking along West Shore Street we saw the Troon StAyles Skiff "Marr Voyager". I made myself known to one of the team officials and enjoyed a long conversation with him. (We have often seen the skiffs and crews practising at Troon whilst overwintering there.) Apparently this year they came last of all at a recent meeting, but did win the award for the eldest crew with a combined age of about 280 years between the 4 of them! Do the maths ... They deserve to win – It's that spirit that saw this country through 2 world wars.

Free Night 239/98

Friday 11th July 2014, "Private Beach" Ullapool, W<3 Very Sunny, Day 633:

We ran out of water in the main tanks last night, so today we decanted the 2 reserve 25 litre Jerry cans and decided to go into the harbour to top up. This we did mid afternoon. The Harbour Master was "cool", he just acknowledged our arrival and made no charge for our visit. As the wind is forecast to rise a little we decided to come south of the moorings where we will have more room to swing, but on the down side we are in 10 – 12 metres at high tide. To compensate for this we are tandem anchored and have 50 metres out on the main rode. A total of 60 metres chain (circa 90kg) and 2 anchors (15lb + 35lb) should be adequate in F4-5.

This morning I went ashore to buy some glue from the hardware shop to mend my walking boots and to watch some of the skiff racing. Like a fool I forgot to take pictures, an oversight I intend to remedy tomorrow. Seeing so many boats not unlike Viking longboats in appearance aggressively forging their way towards the harbour gives what I imagine to be a fairly good impression of what a Viking raid might have looked like.

According to the Ullapool Harbour website [81] there has been a fishing community on this site on the east side of Loch Broom for centuries. Indeed in the 1950s archaeologists found evidence of Viking settlement and some believe that this is how the town got its name Ullapool meaning wool farm. [82] This source also claims that the locals were known as sùlairean which is Gaelic for gannets, the plural form of sùlaire. [83] It is evident that there has been extensive settlement in this area from prehistoric times as can be seen in the number of roundhouses across the region of Wester Ross and Skye. [84] There are 4 roundhouse sites by Ullapool itself pointing to its long history of occupation. It was in 1788 that Ullapool was "officially" founded as a fishing port by the British Fisheries Society [85] a privately funded venture encouraged by the British Government to promote herring fishing in the north and west of Scotland.

"...John Knox proposed that about 50 fishing villages be built in the Highlands containing about 30 or 40 houses with gardens as well as harbours, storehouses, curing sheds, schools, churches etc. These fishing settlements would in turn create work for various tradesmen such as boat builders and craftsmen of various kinds, as well as a focal point for fish curers and merchants." [86]

Angus M[ac]Leod

Ullapool has an interesting recent history too. During the decades between the 1970s and 1990 it was not an uncommon sight to see a large number of factory ships anchored in the loch processing fish, mainly mackerel and herring. These ships became known as klondykers [87] and came from all over the Eastern Block, Western Europe, Egypt and West Africa. Herring stocks began to suffer in the mid 1970s and the British Government imposed a ban on herring fishing and a restriction on foreign vessels fishing within 200 miles of the British coast. The vast majority of mackerel caught in the area by British boats never landed in Ullapool, but was sold directly to the factory ships and exported overseas.

Today Ullapool harbour is still a busy and flourishing port. The main ferry service from the mainland to the outer Hebrides is based here crossing to Stornoway on Lewis, and there is still a local fishing fleet bringing shellfish, crabs, lobsters and scallops as well as seasonally caught whitefish.

A kind local took my line at the jetty and we had a short conversation. He expressed surprise that we had been allowed to anchor where we had between the moorings and the harbour on account of the fishing boats. I said that I had not had a problem with either the fishing boats or the Harbour

Master as I had left enough room for everyone to manoeuvre, but that I did think there are too many moorings. Let's face it, moorings can and should go in deeper water leaving the suitable shallows for anchoring free.

"Lulu Fyffe", a rather large and impressive yacht we know from Troon came in last night. According to a member of staff at Troon he believed that last year only "Lulu Fyffe" and "Quest III" cruised further than us in 2013.

Quest III is the yacht that has achieved fame by being the first yacht to circumnavigate the globe skippered singlehandedly by a deaf person, Gerry Hughes. [88] Gerry is an extraordinary man who would be regarded by any standards as a high achiever. This is to put it mildly! His academic, sporting and charitable achievements are remarkable and the honours he has received are well deserved recognition. In the field of sailing alone he has a number of firsts:

The first deaf skipper to circumnavigate the British Isles, in 1981.

The first deaf skipper to sail across the Atlantic Ocean in the Original Single-Handed Transatlantic Race, OSTAR, 2005.

And, on 8th May 2013 arrived back in Troon to become, the first Deaf Yachtsman to solo circumnavigate the globe via the Five Great Capes.

This evening Nick and Linda arrived with the caravan so we had tea with them. We left the dogs aboard and they behaved perfectly.

(Homemade Pizza)   *Free Night 240/99*

Saturday 12th July 2014, "Private Beach" Ullapool, Rain S1-2, Day 634:

Today is Henry David Thoreau's birthday (1817); he'd have been 197 years old!

This was a most enjoyable day during which there was great entertainment provided by the Scottish Coastal Rowing Association race meeting. I went along to support the Troon team. The highlight of the day, however, was a visit to my musician friend Stephen's house. Years ago we had worked together and it was a joy to be reunited.

Sunday 13th July 2014, "Private Beach" Ullapool, S<2 Overcast, Day 635:

Claire and I spent the day with Nick and Linda at the caravan park with the dogs. Mid afternoon I came back to Drumlin with the dogs and Claire returned to Dingwall with Nick and Linda and our laundry!

I spent the evening aboard and listened to BBC Radio 5 Live's coverage of the Germany v Argentina football World Cup Final. Germany just managed a goal in the closing minutes of extra time preventing a penalty shoot out finish. I felt sorry for the Argentineans who had a number of good opportunities but somehow failed to follow through with them. What a dilemma! Which team to support when both countries have been our enemy in war? Perhaps we should sort all our political problems out with sport instead of guns! On the other hand we would probably lose!!

(Fish and Chips from the shop)   *Free Night 242/101*

129

Monday 14th July 2014, Private Beach Ullapool, S<2 Overcast, Day 636:

I fixed the shower tray pump today, as it had stopped working, by disconnecting the waste pipe at the pump end and sending some water under pressure back through it using a washing up liquid bottle. It worked and dislodged the blockage.

The Church of England today voted to allow women to become Bishops at the Synod held in York.

(Vegetable Stew and Dumplings)   Free Night 243/102

Wednesday 16th July 2014, Private Beach Ullapool, Overcast and Showers, Day 638:

This morning I went for a musical session at Stephen's house at the head of the loch today with another friend of his called Alan, a drummer. A good time was had by all; Stephen even talked me into singing a couple of rock songs!

Claire and I spent the afternoon quietly on the boat while the squalls passed over. Our friend Elizabeth is coming tomorrow.

Other news - The "domestic" battery is dead and in urgent need of charging.

(Chili)   Free Night 245/104

Thursday 17th July 2014, Private Beach Ullapool, Sunny and Fair, Day 639:

Elizabeth was our guest for the day and I went ashore this morning for 5 litres of petrol, some shopping from the supermarket and to collect her from the harbour pier. We sailed Drumlin down through the narrows of Loch Broom and tacked back to the anchorage; 5nm and 3 hours of sailing and only 40 minutes using the motor. The anchors didn't snag that nasty little submerged buoy either. Phew!

The 15kg gas bottle was empty this morning; it has taken 3 months and at £35 that works out at about 30 pence per day. I managed to replace it at the local garage which fortunately is close enough to not involve too much heavy weight carrying.

We plan to set sail for Stornoway tomorrow.

(Salad and Ham)   *Free Night 246/105*

CHAPTER SEVEN

The Language Barrier

"Go to, let us go down, and there confound
their language, that they may not
understand one another's
speech." [89]

Friday 18th July 2014, Stornoway, E4 Sunny, Day 640:
*We sailed practically all the way from Ullapool today,
initially very steadily and in blazing sunshine, and as the day
progressed the wind increased. We saw numerous fishing
boats, a Royal Navy ship and a wake! We assume it was the
submarine we had heard about on the VHF radio heading for
the Raasay exercise area. There were also a noticeable
number of puffins, fulmars and Bonxies around today.*

(Salad)   *Free Night 247/106*

I wish they'd just let me be!

Life lived in parenthesis,
Bracketed and set apart,
Living amanuensis,
Dictated to from the start.

Draped in crude quotation marks,
Forced to wear words not my own,
Made to veil my vital spark,
Hid, the true me never known.

Oppressed by the great repressed,
Suppressed by unjust decree,
Depressed by false social mores,
I wish they'd just let me be!

Andrew Dalby, Stornoway, 19th July 2014

Sunday 20th July 2014, Arnish Stornoway, Overcast S3-4,
Day 642:
*It has been a cool and drizzly day. At lunch time we
motored the dinghy to the marina. We had a wander around
and checked out the town anchorage by Tesco. It looks
tenable so we may mooch up in the morning at low tide and
try it out. We have done little else today. I sorted out a
"project" poem and divided it into two poems and" finished"
them off.*

(Pizza & Salad)   Free Night 249/108

It is Written

"It is written", so we're told,
Brow beaten by pious men,
"In the scriptures, its The Word!"
Tell me!
Which god ere held a pen?

Written large upon our hearts,
Rules and laws, those manmade chains
Hold us down so we allow
Priests and kings to hold the reins.

133

Our minds and bodies stolen,
Made slaves to aid their purpose,
Our wills destroyed or broken,
Like clowns in Mammon's circus.

Pacified, conditioned thus,
Giving not a second thought,
We labour for our masters,
Knowing not how much we're caught.

What is right they say is wrong,
And wrongs they make a virtue,
They take away our freedoms,
Give privilege to the few.

The fact is WE are guilty,
We flatter them with our votes,
It matters not who's captain,
We're sinking in the same sad boat!

The State serves not the people,
Democracy is dead! [90]
The system worships money,
By corporate greed is led.

We can't cut off this monster's head,
Like the Hydra more will grow, [91]
The time has come, let us now
Strike at its roots below.

Rise up! Resist! Don't give in,
There is another way!
Deny them the power they wield,
By refusing to obey!

Civil disobedience, [92]
Passive aggression, be clear!
We don't have to live this way,
And all that stops us is fear!

Andrew Dalby, Stornoway, 20th July 2014

This poem is about anarchy in its truest and purest form. People in charge of their own lives not domesticated by the State and used as pit ponies in the money mines of the economy which serves greed not people. The justification for all State power is rooted in the morals of religion, the ally of tyranny. Religion, it seems to me, is manmade, but I choose to believe in God nevertheless. That is a personal choice. Separate God from religion and moral authority is taken away from those that use this or that scripture to claim advantageous positions exclusively for themselves. Religion is divisive, favours the powerful institutions of church and State over people and gives the few privilege and power unfairly over the rest. This is a situation that needs continually challenging.

The argument will be that the law, police and military will be used against such refusal. Yes, but if the individuals within these institutions heed the same call, there is no lawyer, police officer, civil servant or soldier to do the State's dirty work. It starts with the individual, with you, with me. When there are enough we will prevail.

Tuesday 22nd July 2014, Red Rocks Stornoway, Sunny SE1, Day 644:
I went ashore to explore and to try out the repair to my walking boots. I discovered the giant Co-op and a post office and garage near to it at the north end of town. My boots

survived. I didn't find a music shop and Tesco is so close it is not worth trying the Co-op a mile or more away.

(Bean Stew & Dumplings)   *Free Night 251/110*

Thursday 24th July 2014, Red Rocks Stornoway, Very Sunny, Day 646:

We have roasted today again in glorious sunshine. My new glasses broke last night and the optician here can't fix them. I rang the optician who supplied them and they say a new pair are needed, so I am back to wearing my old glasses until we visit Thirsk in November!

We did very little today. I went ashore twice to take and collect my spectacles and Claire took a walk into town before tea time.

(Pizza & Salad)   *Free Night 253/112*

Friday 25th July 2014, Red Rocks Stornoway, Very Sunny 31°C in the shade, Day 646:

Claire insisted that I get the bus today and go west. I was not sure about doing this as the local tourist information leaflets and bus timetables are ambiguous enough to test the veterans of Bletchley Park. I did, however, acquiesce and took the W2 service at 10.10 to the Doune Broch. I had 28 minutes to locate, visit and return to the road end bus stop for the next leg of the bus journey. It is an impressive structure deserving of at least an hour's attention, but I saw it. It is remarkable that one can still enter inside the walls and climb the 2000 year old steps within. The quality and position on the escarpment of the dry stone walling is impressive too.

Brochs are enigmatic edifices, exclusively Scottish, double walled, made of drystone and circular, whose roofing and uses are a matter of conjecture and the subject of a lot of debate amongst experts as to their exact function. It is disputed whether they were intended as fortifications, or as farms, or just residences, but many believe that they were Iron Age high status dwellings, tough though not necessarily primarily defensive. What cannot be denied is the superlative quality of the drystone craftsmanship that was required to build them. There are many sites which date from anywhere between 300BC and 100AD, mainly around the north and west of Scotland, though few are as complete as Dun Carloway.

I returned to Callanish Stones, the Stone Henge of the Isles. This is a strange piece of antiquity occupying a good acre or more of land. Cruciform in shape, it predates most of Judeo Christian history, being 5000 years old.

There are many megalithic stone circles around northwest Europe some of which have known astronomical significance, but many, like Callanish Stones, are not fully understood, if at all. Some believe that they may have been built as exercises in community cohesion or for religious purposes. What is known is that Callanish was used as a burial site, but beyond that little is certain. Whatever these stones were erected for, it was certainly a massive undertaking requiring the cooperation, organisation and pure strength of a great many people.

Saturday 26th July 2014, Red Rocks Stornoway, Variable 2-4 Rain Warm, Day 648:
The weather broke today and we have had some quite heavy rain. I did the shopping, two big provisioning trips to stock up on storables for the 2nd part of our voyage down "The Long Isle". We have been considering, but have concluded that a trip out to St Kilda is not an option with the 2 dogs; they don't like rolling sea or long passages and that trip would offer both in spade loads! Pity! So close yet so far...

We have used our 50 litres of spare water so a top up is required tomorrow after which the weather will determine our progress south.

After yesterday's excursion to the broch and standing stones out west I managed to compose a couple of poems today, one about the broch (an acrostic with an ABCBA rhyme scheme that on the page implies the shape of a broch), and a sonnet for the standing stones.

(Chili)   *Free Night 255/114*

Dun Carloway Broch

Before the deeds of men in script found fame,

Reminders took their places on the land.

On craggy rocks and mountain tops,

Creations in remembrance stand, and

Honour still those folk we cannot name.

Andrew Dalby, Stornoway, 25 July 2014

-oOo-

"Edifices, either standing or ruined,
are the chief records of an
illiterate nation." [93]
Samuel Johnson

Callanish Stones

Five thousand years these giant stones have stood,
A testament to ancient ways now past,
Erected here with tears, with sweat and blood,
We have the scene, but have not plot nor cast.

An avenue leads south onto this stage,
Outstretched are arms one each to east and west,
But in that central circus is no page
Of dialogue with meaning to divest.

Directions have we none to teach us how
On this arena's set to act or dance!
Or should we sing, or pray, or say our vows,
Or read the moon and stars and trust to chance?

Oh standing stones of Callanish so grey,
Today we strain to hear the words you say.

Andrew Dalby, Stornoway, 26 July 2014

Sunday 27th July 2014, Red Rocks Stornoway, Rain / Overcast, Day 649:

We had torrential rain this morning, but after lunch it faired up so we weighed anchor and went along side the marina pontoons to take on water. The young harbour master was most kind and pointed out all the facilities allowing us to stay alongside whilst we used the showers (£1 for 6 minutes). There was no berthing charge for a short stay. In conversation we told him that we anchor and were intending to return to Arnish for tonight, but he said it was a "private" pier and that we should go back to into Red Rocks and warned us it can be shoal. I think he was concerned about the big ships turning round at the pier which we have experienced without issues.

On the way round to the marina one of the local seals came to investigate the dogs and he rose out of the water and spat at Bracken scaring the life out of him and splashed back into the depths. It was quite funny, but the question what he would have done to Chip or Bracken if they had gone into the water doesn't bear thinking about! Seals are big beasts...

We have used the engine so little that the number 2 domestic battery went flat today. Hopefully the 1 ½ hours the engine was allowed to run today has revived it. I am so glad our anchor light is a 3Watt L.E.D. (25Watt equivalent) lamp. Anything is better than the wind up garden lamp we had to use last year!

141

Sterna hirundo, [94] *or terns as they are better known, are entertaining little birds and have been frolicking around us at Red Rocks all week performing aerial acrobatics, squabbling over the proceeds of hunting and generally engaging in rough and tumble. As the light fades it is not unlike watching bats in flight. This evening 3 terns visited our cockpit, but 1 remained perched on the life ring for perhaps 10 minutes. He was almost certainly aware of my presence in the saloon as we had a clear line of sight of each other. I was inspired to write a poem using alliteration and assonance to mimic their antics tonight!*

(Oaty Bake)   *Free Night 256/115*

Monday 28 July 2014, Loch Grimshader, Overcast S/SW1-2, Day 650:
We left Stornoway before lunch and sailed most of the 3 – 4 miles to Loch Grimshader into which it was best to motor as it is so confined and hazardous. Besides the wind was coming right down the Loch! It is well worth coming in as it is a lovely sheltered anchorage and very quiet. There is a community here, however, probably a couple of dozen houses. There are also a few boats along the Loch, mainly work boats, but there are a couple of Westerly Centaurs, smaller sisters of Drumlin.

The Tern

Twisting turning learning every breath of breeze
You please to tease and weave with ease
On wings that cling you wind and find
The lift and drift to soar before
You lunge and plunge to catch a fish
The dish on which you dine from time to time
The food to feed the broods you breed

And so you agile acrobatic bird
Fly high the sky in ballet herds
And dance and prance with flair in air so fair
And twist and turn and learn the breeze
And please to tease and weave with ease
On wings that cling you wind and find
The lift and drift to soar above the earth below
Is how I know is how I learn by every turn
You are a tern!

Andrew Dalby, Loch Grimshader 28th July 2014

Tuesday 29th July 2014, Loch Grimshader, Showers W/SW5-6, Day 651:
The wind today has pinned us down and is forecast to stay the same tomorrow too, so we shall be staying put for a while. We have read a lot. There is no phone or internet signal.

(Vegetable Pie and Potatoes)   *Free Night 258/117*

Thursday 31st July 2014, Loch Thorasdaidh Erisort, Sunny NE1-2, Day 653:
We decided to head south and came into the rather awkward to navigate Loch Erisort. We only have an Imray Chart (Not a particularly detailed chart) *and pilot book for these waters so much dead slow manoeuvring with me on the bows rock spotting whilst Claire steered was required. We finally made it into this beautiful little anchorage between Toa and En Chalium Chille (Collumba's Church). Indeed there is a church right on the shore complete with graveyard and headstones.*

I went ashore to investigate and discovered a church, a pier, a spring, 2 cairns, some standing stones, various archaeological ruined buildings and the chassis and engine of a very old truck inside a walled enclosure. I even removed a bucket from the head of a sheep! Somehow the silly ovine had put its head through the bottom of a broken black plastic pail and was wandering around like some surreal animated 1960's object d'art furry lamp complete with black lampshade head gear and black stockings. Pretty, functional or elegant it was not, but owing to its extremely narrow field of vision I managed to walk right up to it, grab the adornment and with a quick flick of the wrist (and a tug from the lamb) removed the offending receptacle. The lamb seemed none the worse, but in truth it would have starved to death had I not intervened.

I think I may go ashore tomorrow to try to make some sense of the archaeology and to read some of the headstones. One I saw today seemed to read ,"Penelope aged 51 beloved wife of Rev. John McRae..."

(Pizza)   *Free Night 260/119*

Friday 1st August 2014, Loch Thorasdaidh Erisort, Sunshine and Showers Variable 2, Day 654:
I climbed up the hill on the island to find some phone signal. I managed to contact civilisation, just. On the way down I looked at some of the graves in the ruined church; the only 2 legible memorials were for ladies, both 34 years old, who died in the late 1800s circa 1870. Later than I had anticipated given the state of the ruins.

The following is taken from the notes I made in the graveyard:

In Memory of Isabella Martin
Wife of Angus McLean Lewerbo [*Sic*] [95]
Who died 12th June 1870
Aged 34 Years

-oOo-

Placed by Murdo Morrison Laxay
In memory of his beloved wife
Anabella McLeod Who died
29 September Aged 34 Years [96]

-oOo-

In Memory of Penelope wife of the
Rev John McRea of Loch ...
Whe ...[indecipherable] ...   Jesus on
9th December ??90
Aged 54 years.

(Soup and Dumplings)   *Free Night 261/120*

Saturday 2nd August 2014, Loch Thorasdaidh Erisort, Rain
N/NE 5-8, Day 655:
*The weather has arrived! We are hunkered down for the
next few days as this low passes northwards over us. We feel a
bit out of it here. Although this is a good, sheltered anchorage
we are out of the way, and all that we have is the VHF radio if
anything goes wrong. We are also feeling a long way from
home. An ironic situation given that home is where Drumlin
is. I think the lack of ability to keep in touch with family plays
a large part in these feelings. Maybe this is an unusual
manifestation of loneliness!*

*Other news -I have finished re-reading another one of my
old college set texts today and started yet another which I
have waded 25% of the way through. It is amazing how much
I have forgotten, or what I missed as a youngster! I am
benefitting more out of these re-readings now probably*

because I have better general knowledge than I had back then along with a more mature and settled disposition better suited to wrestling with heavy texts!

It is a shame that there are so many sheep about as we can't take the dogs ashore. Yesterday, whilst I was ashore, Claire witnessed my little terrier Chip doing the most amazing thing; he was attempting to mimic the sound of the sheep bleating! Not once, but sustained attempts in response to the lambs on the shore.

Claire baked 2 cakes today; lemon and chocolate chip.

(Pasta & Hotdog Sausages)   *Free Night 262/121*

Sunday 3rd August 2014, Loch Thorasdaidh Erisort, Calm and Sunny, Day 656:
We endured a very windy and rainy night with F8 northerly or NE gales until about 6am. I stayed up most of the night and Claire didn't sleep well. Today has been a lull, and even some hot sunshine, though more wind is forecast for tonight and tomorrow bringing the winds round to the south. Precisely the direction we want to go! Hey ho!

We spent the day catching up on sleep, reading and listening to the radio. A thunder storm passed over rumbling but it didn't let loose. Phew ...

(Salad)   *Free Night 263/122*

Lewis Haiku

Once a sovereign state
Now the Long Isle's autumn years?
Make languages borders!

A Dalby, Loch Thorasdaidh, Erisort. 3rd August 2014

I have been contemplating the issue of Scottish Independence recently as an outside observer on the inside. Although I live nomadically in Scotland I do not, of course, have the right to vote in the referendum as I do not live in a house. Even if I did I would not vote, I am not Scottish, neither do I have any vested interests in the outcome of the referendum. In short, it is nothing to do with me! I am interested in the whole concept of sovereignty though. In recent decades there has been a big debate in British politics about Economic and Monetary Union and many politicians and commentators argued that to relinquish Sterling in favour of the Euro was tantamount to relinquishing sovereignty and by implication our culture. There may have been real concerns about some loss of control over some aspects of financial and political issues, but in reality there was never any threat to our culture. History is littered with good examples of how cultures are wiped out, and almost without exception the aggressors seek to prevent or undermine the use of one's native tongue and other ethnic denominators if they differ from those of the conquering force. This is easily achieved by choosing to impose their own language as the lingua franca of officialdom and education.

I lived and studied in Wales when I was a student. As a 19 year old I was surprised to learn from my Welsh friends that there are native born people on the mainland of Great Britain fluent in their indigenous mother tongue which is not English, and that there were even some who cannot speak English! I quickly learnt that culture is an inherent part of, if not consequence of, language. Language is the vehicle for ideas, it reflects or mirrors the personality of a people in the rhythm and tone of the vernacular which in turn shapes and defines its literature, poetry and song; it is not necessarily a product of a particular place. Welsh is alive and well, in spite of the hegemony of the Anglophone system. I am always very heartened when I see and hear Welsh being used as this means the culture of Wales is able to thrive.

I came to the Outer Hebrides eagerly anticipating that I would hear much Gaelic being spoken as ubiquitously as I hear Welsh when in Wales. I was so excited by this prospect because I have never heard it spoken except on the radio and television; never in real life. Imagine my profound disappointment when it took several days in and around Stornoway before I heard a word of it spoken. Why does this matter? It matters because some in Scotland want to regain independence, but what is it that they think they are retrieving from their old adversaries the English? I think it unlikely that Gaelic would be made the official language and that the schools will educate their pupils in it. Will they insist on mitigating the effects of the 1746 Act of Proscription by insisting on the wearing of the kilt, the restoration of the clan system or the right to bear arms? I began to feel that the people with most to lose in Scotland are those who still live in a culture where Gaelic is the first language and that they should perhaps be seeking to be independent of all the rest of us English speakers. There seems to me to be a very real danger that Scotland is losing its true heritage. Do not be fooled by the proliferation of Gaelic on road signs, it is cosmetic window dressing compared with what really needs to be done. We should all care about Scotland, above all we should care about the Gaelic language and encourage it to grow and flourish. We should cherish and celebrate this precious language for the unique culture it has given us in the form of all of the Scottish people.

> "There is no tracing the connection of ancient nations, but
> by language; and therefore I am always sorry
> when any language is lost, because
> languages are the pedigree
> of nations." [97]
> Samuel Johnson

Monday 4th August 2014, Loch Thorasdaidh Erisort, SW 4-6 Overcast, Day 657:
Today it is the centenary of the British entry into the 1st World War!

(Curry)   *Free Night 264/123*

Thursday 7th August 2014, Scalpay North Harbour, S3 Sunshine and Showers, Day 660:
I went ashore this morning to check out the landing, it was ok by the slip, but no good by the steps by the pier. I visited the shop and was made very welcome by the young man serving. I bought bread rolls and burgers as we are both craving protein!

This afternoon we went ashore with the dogs to take them for a long walk. On arriving at the slip a gentleman was just offloading his catch from an open boat which he has on a pulley mooing a few yards out in the harbour. We got talking to him and he insisted that we help ourselves to his biggest mackerel; we took 2 and he insisted we take more. We took 2 more. We know from experience that we can't eat more than 2 each. Result? This evening we feasted and again felt full. Mackerel has the effect of making us feel full.

The dogs enjoyed their walk around this beautiful village with its houses nestled on all levels on the hilly island around the 2 harbours, north and south, which are just yards apart. We went into the shop to buy fresh new potatoes for our tea. I was holding the fish in a plastic carrier bag, and when a local lady stood beside me I said to her that if there was a smell of fish it was me! A short conversation arose about how we'd met this really kind gentleman who had provided us with our tea when without warning the said benefactor emerged around the corner from the other aisle!

At the side of the road leading onto the pier there is a local information board which provides interesting facts about this enchanting little island:

Scalpay is a close-knit community of some three hundred and fifty inhabitants, most of whom are related. The main industries on the island are fishing and fish farming although weaving and crafting is also carried out ... Both North and South Harbours provide safe natural anchorage for boats. At the turn of the century there were a number of curing stations on the island, and at one time many fishermen worked from 38 boats.

The houses and cars to be seen along the road are testimony to the years of economic prosperity enjoyed by the island in the 20th century.

Beyond Kennavay you can get a clear view of Skye, and of the offshore rocks where the cargo ship "Golf Star" ran aground in 1996.

Charles Edward Stuart sought refuge on Scalpay for a while when he was fleeing after the battle of Culloden in 1746. Local tradition tells that he hid in the cave in the secluded spot at Lag an Laine ... The lighthouse on Eilean Glas was completed in 1789 the first project undertaken by the Northern Lighthouse Trust after its establishment by Act of Parliament in 1786. It was automated in 1976 ... Loch an Duin [has] the remains of [a] prehistoric island dun or fort ...

I was amused to read the part that says, "most of whom are related" because my sister in law Linda is something of an amateur genealogist and has spent many years researching her family tree in great depth. Her investigations have brought her to this area of the Hebrides many times, and on an early visit she soon discovered she was related to the landlady of the guest house she was staying in!

-oOo-

On the down side, the diesel pump on the pier is not working at the moment and there does not appear to be water on the pier. It looks like a trip to Tarbert will be necessary unless we can find a way around it. There are also gales forecast for early next week from the north or northwest, so we may relocate to another anchorage, but we'd like to make contact with Heather first. (Heather and her husband John are old friends from Yorkshire who have a cottage just over the bridge on Harris.)

We have been joined this evening at anchor by "Fat Chance" a yacht we suspect we have seen before, but we are unsure where.

(Mackerel with New Potatoes)   *Fee Night 267/126*

There is something about the idea of a ship that is made of concrete that seems just wrong! It is counterintuitive to think that something with the properties of stone can float. We blithely accept that ships made of metal float, but cement floating jars with reason. But there have been many ships made of cement and *Cretetree* is one. She is now designated as a hulk, a ship stripped of fittings and used as storage, and she resides in North Harbour on the island of Scalpay. I paid her a visit on Friday 8th August where I met a local school boy who knew what it was and was quite unmoved by it. It was just there, a commonplace part of his life and he seemed to see nothing out of the ordinary in it!

Cretetree was built in Aberdeen in 1918 by a firm founded by James Scott and Son called the Aberdeen Concrete Shipbuilding Company. [98] She is 55.19 metres long, 9.6 metres wide and 5.79 metres deep and has a gross registered tonnage of 711. Her official number is 143055 and her construction yard number was 1. She was commissioned by the Shipping Controller of London as PD146 and named *Cretetree*. They later transferred her to The Board of Trade in 1921. Between 1922 and 1928 she was owned by the Crete Shipping Company of London (Stelp and Leighton Ltd.) who sold her to John W Robertson of Lerwick who kept her until 1948 when W A Bruce of Stornoway took her on until she was deleted from the Lloyd register in 1955. She was finally laid up in Scalpay to be used as a fisherman's jetty and store where she remains to this day, although sadly awash and no longer floating. In her working life she was a barge for carrying coal [99] and it is believed that during World War 2 she was at Scapa Flow. She was never equipped with an engine and would have had to be towed by another vessel.

I was really overwhelmed by a strange sensation as I approached this leviathan. It was unnerving! I could feel a presence, a VERY strong presence. This is not a new experience for me and one I am sure many of us have had somewhere and at some stage in our life. *Cretetree* is made of the same stuff, and is about the same size, as a small terrace of houses. What makes her different? Perhaps it is the fact that she is not rooted to the ground; she is a moveable object. I don't know. I am aware of similar sensations whenever I am around very large manmade objects like steam engines, aeroplanes or lorries; it is a feeling commensurate to that which I feel in a church, a cathedral or a cave. Whatever it is that I am sensitive to; all I can say is that it is very real and otherworldly. It reassures me that there are things we cannot explain. It reassures me that there is a spiritual dimension to the physical world.

The Presence

Some feel the closeness of primeval force
When stood before great works of human kind,
Unnatural giants wrought by hands of men
And fashioned while the sweat dripped from their brow.

A ship, a church, machines of many sorts,
Infused with life do radiate abroad
Vitality, a power from within.
Did those who built them leave some soul behind?

Should one interpret from that ghostly sense
This as the presence of Almighty God
In man's creations, monuments to craft?
Or does another spirit there reside?

Andrew Dalby, Dunvegan, 17th August 2014

Saturday 9th August 2014, Scalpay, S4 Sunny, Day 662:
We enjoyed the company of a lovely Danish couple at
teatime this evening. Felice and Bjarne were on their way to
Orkney where they were to lay up their boat for winter and
return to Denmark. They are a young couple, younger than us,

and semi-retired due to the success they had in business. Rather than avariciously pursuing ever greater wealth they decided to enjoy the riches of travel and time together.

Earlier in the day I walked over the Scalpay Bridge which links the island to Harris and I began to ponder a mystery that had its genesis when we were on Raasay. I wrote the following memo to myself on my mobile phone for future consideration:

> A matter that has been present in my thoughts, though not worked through is this... Raasay has a £10million ferry "Hallaig" to serve an island of 161 [100] residents. They spent £6.4 million on Scalpay bridge for an island of about 291 (2011) [101] inhabitants. Both communities have schools, yet Rowen village school in North Wales for example was, I believe, shut on cost grounds. Funny what government will spend on and what it won't... Discuss!

It is worth noting that the Wikipedia entries for both these islands suggest a population decrease during a time of increase in the islands overall.

Raasay's ferry MV Hallaig [102] is the first ever hybrid ferry in the world and is one of a pair to be built by Ferguson Shipbuilders in Port Glasgow at a combined cost of £20 million. Hallaig was launched in December 2012 and is operated by Caledonian M^{ac}Brayne, owned by Caledonian

Maritime Assets which is ultimately owned by the Scottish Government. She entered service in 2013. Some of the funding for the ship came from the European Regional Development Fund.

I copied the following information from the road sign by the bridge from Harris to Scalpay:

"The Western Isles Council Scalpay Bridge

This project has been partly financed by the European Regional Development Fund under the Highlands and Islands Objective One Partnership Programme"

According to the ERDF (European Regional Development Fund" website:

"The EDFR aims to strengthen economic and social cohesion in the European Union by correcting imbalances between its regions." [103]

And it goes on to say:

"Areas that are naturally disadvantaged from a geographical viewpoint (remote, mountainous or sparsely populated areas) benefit from special treatment. Lastly, the outermost areas also benefit from specific assistance from the ERDF to address possible disadvantages due to their remoteness."

The Comhairle nan Eilean Siar website [104] states that The Europen Union contributed £4.2 million from the ERDF, that is 65% of the total £6.4 million cost, for the bridge making the project viable. The 170 metre long box girder structure (which was made in the Netherlands!) was opened on 16th December 1997.

The bridge is clearly what the locals wanted and has been beneficial to them, but unlike some of the ferry services it does not appear to me that there is anything on the other side (i.e. Harris) to undermine the integrity of the island's community, unlike for example Gigha whose residents can take the ferry to shop in Campbeltown on the mainland or even Raasay where residents can easily leave the island for life's basic needs in Portree on Skye. Perhaps bridges do less harm than ferries, but then again where does that leave Skye?

What I find frustrating is that vast sums of money can be found for THINGS such as bridges and ferries, but there is a miserly short-sightedness in the accountancy when relatively small amounts of public money cannot be found to support PEOPLE in the form of local services like schools, medical facilities or shops which could preserve small village communities. I think that some local government areas seem to have their priorities wrong. It also seems to me that implicit in these "improvements" that "correct" is evidence that the official view that the remoteness of these places is a disadvantage; disadvantageous to whom? The disadvantages may, perhaps, be a point of view or an opinion, but they are certainly not universal facts. Remoteness may be a distinct advantage and in my view is something to be highly prized on a vastly overpopulated island like Britain. Here we have an example of state sponsored urbanite bureaucracy's idea that civilisation and the state are inherently superior to that which is untouched and undefiled by it. You will also not that at the top of the list for the ERDF is "economic" cohesion. For these people value is only something that is measured in financial terms. At its worst this attitude is most keenly observed in the dreadful forced contact inflicted upon many uncontacted tribes around the world who do not wish to be assimilated.

Sunday 10th August 2014, Scalpay North Harbour, Sunny then Overcast Var 1-2, Day 663:
It is our 29th Wedding Anniversary!

We have had a quiet day. Scalpay, predictably for a Scottish Free Church island, has been virtually dead with little activity save a couple of dog walkers and the cars to and from the church services. The weather is slowly cooling and degrading as the remnants of hurricane Bertha approach the coast, and we are waiting for it to pass and for more seasonal weather with a north or west component in the wind so that we can head east and south to Skye; probably Dunvegan then Harport and the Small Isles.

This evening we had a call from Heather, our friend with the house at Kyle Scalpay; she has arrived safely and has kindly invited us round tomorrow evening.

This morning Claire made a full English breakfast of hot dog sausages, eggs, tomatoes, beans and bread for our slap up celebration meal to mark the commencement of our 30th year of matrimony, followed by a batch of scones for afternoon tea. (The real celebration of our wedding anniversary was on 20th June at Shieldaig Lodge!)

(Full English Breakfast)   *Free Night 270/129*

Monarchs of the Glens

Walking through the fern and heather,
There live the herds of deer,
And mighty antlers crown their heads,
Their majesty so clear.

And sitting on her rocky throne,
There lives the jewelled viper,
Queen with diamonds set down her back,
There's nothing else quite like her.

And in the silvery streams that flow,
There live the princely trout,
Who dance and play amongst the stones,
And swim and leap about.

And hiding in their hillside dens,
There live the ermined stoats,
Lords and Ladies of the land,
Resplendent in their coats.

And soaring high above them all,
There lives the golden eagle,
Reigns on gliding wings outstretched,
King of birds so regal.

Andrew Dalby, Scalpay 10th August 2014

Initially I conceived this as another children's poem to be accompanied by pictures to go with "They Can't See Me" and "Jilly the Jellyfish". This is what came, and a royalty theme grew within it. It is for primary school aged children. I could devise a whole term's topic out of this poem and the painting it evokes and parodies its name on... Alas I'm retired so others will have to deliver those lessons on my behalf! Once a teacher, always a teacher.

Tuesday 12th August 2014, Scalpay North Harbour, NW 4-5 Overcast & Showers, Day 665:
I walked the dogs this morning and brought 20 litres of water aboard. This afternoon our friend Heather kindly picked us up and took us back to her holiday cottage at Kyle for supper and showers; we had a lovely time catching up and finding out about mutual friends and the general goings on in Thirsk and Sowerby, our old home. Sadly John, Heather's husband, is unable to be with us as he has not yet returned home from his business trip to the States. It is a pity as we would have enjoyed going for a sail with him. The dogs were well behaved whilst we were away.

Last night was very windy. I stayed up until 5.30am monitoring our position. We swept over a rock or some other underwater obstruction a few times grinding the port keel. I tried to haul in some chain, but the wind was too strong and engine power would have been required so we stayed put. We connected 2 or 3 times with the obstruction but not with any great force and the tide was soon rising again. This morning I reduced the anchor chain from 45 to 35 metres and sent the angel down. The winds have eased.
Free Night 272/131

Wednesday 13th August 2014, Scalpay North Harbour, NW2-3 Overcast, Day 666:
I filled the water tank this morning and did a shopping trip. In the afternoon Chip and I walked up to the loch to see the dun (Crannog).

(Tuna Pasta)   *Free Night 273/132*

CHAPTER EIGHT

War and Weather

"Dulce et decorum est pro patria mori". [105]

Thursday 14th August 2014, Dunvegan, W3 Fai, Day 667:
Today is Neil's birthday; he would have been 23 years old.
(For anyone reading this who has not read *373 Days Afloat*,
Neil was our second son who died aged 9 following a long
battle against leukaemia in 2000.)

*The Coast Guard Maritime Safety Information (CGMSI)
broadcast courtesy of the Met Office forecast N or NW 4-5
occasionally 6. We left Scalpay in dead calm and had to
motor for quite a few hours before we could reasonably sail.
When we did sail it was in a light westerly. It is beyond a joke
now how many times, and how consistently, the forecasts are
significantly wrong and bear NO similarity to the actual
weather in the areas they forecast for! Gale warnings are
trustworthy; nothing else can be relied upon and the short
term (i.e. the day's forecast and the following 24 hours)
precludes any meaningful long term view essential in passage
planning. This is why we use a web site called
www.xcweather.co.uk and only bother with the coast guard
broadcast for amusement; cross-referencing weather facts
and the for safety information such as when HMS Sneaky
Warfare is practising shooting torpedoes or 23 Regiment Big
Guns are lobbing missiles off the cliffs out to sea.*

*It is good to be making progress south now and to be back
in connection with Johnson and Boswell's Journey around the
Hebrides.*

"Here ... we settled, and did not spoil the
present hour with thoughts
of departure." [106]
Samuel Johnson

*For some reason Dunvegan Castle is not at all like I
imagined, I think I had expected a much more austere, even
Gothic, castle taller than its footprint and in a remote and
isolated place perched on the far end of a spit of land. It is ¾
mile or so from quite a large village, and more country house
shaped than castle in a well sheltered loch. Still, in Johnson's
time the area and castle would perhaps have conformed more
to my fantasy than the present reality.*

(Chile Con Veggie)   *Fee night 274/133*

Friday 15th August 2014, Dunvegan, NW2 Overcast/Fair, Day 668:

We slept well and the anchor held, the wind was calm all night, so it should have. This morning we inflated the dinghy and went ashore with the dogs for a walk and to check out the local amenities. There are a couple of shops for provisions and the garage is a 5 minute walk from the jetty at Dunvegan Hotel.

This afternoon I walked to Dunvegan castle with a view to taking a roadside picture and finding out the entry fee. Having arrived at the gate which was all roped off with a fancy ticket office staffed by a smartly liveried lady behind the glass, like a teller in a bank, I felt myself rapidly relapsing into indignation and rage. Last Christmas I wrote a trilogy of poems on the 3 wise men, baby Jesus and presents theme, and today I found those sentiments resounding again as I walked through the car park where all us common folks gather before being asked to pay £10 each to visit the seat of the Clan M^{ac}Leod, and thereby subsidise the upkeep of an hereditary landowner's house. The relatively poor propping up the rich in short!

I was reminded of how Lady M^{ac}Leod complained of the hardships of living at Dunvegan, and I must confess to a severe lack of sympathy. Something I think I share with Mr Boswell!

> "The lady insisted that the rock was very inconvenient;
> that there was no place near it where a good
> garden could be made; that it must always
> be the rude place; that it was a
> Herculean labour to make
> dinner here." [107]
> James Boswell

163

I am quite sure the clan chief does not struggle on minimum wage for 40 hours plus each week to scrape together enough to pay his rent, feed his children, and heat his house. It is more likely that he enjoys significant revenue from his estate in rents received and produce raised upon it to fuel a lifestyle of luxury only dreamed of by most of us. Walking back I thought about the phrase we use about "How the other half live". These gentry are not the other half; for every one of them there are thousands of us. Let us say they number about 600 (i.e. the Peers in the House of Lords) and there are about 60,000,000 people in the United Kingdom, that works out at 1 gent per 100,000 peasants. So, the other half? No! The other 0.0001% of the population. Much as I would like to see the castle for its historic significance, I, as a relatively poor member of that 100,000 majority group, do not feel inclined to prop up the finances of the privileged minority.

*I stomped the ¾ mile back to Dunvegan village hoping that healthy exercise would calm the rage. By the time I arrived at the village I felt calmer and decided to visit the newly lit war memorial via its new access path. Upon reaching the small enclosure containing the column with the names of the "Glorious Dead" my mood was immediately insulted again, like a poke in a recent wound, on 2 accounts. The first thing that struck me was that those commemorated were listed by rank, officers above privates, as if they had superiority in death as in life! I was immediately finding myself asking why we do not list the dead in the order they died? In all likelihood the lower ranks died by following the orders of the class of person listed above. Secondly, as I walked round to the front of the memorial, the front face proclaimed that most vile of propagandist insults to the intelligence, "The Glorious Dead"! **THERE IS NO GLORY***

IN BEING DEAD**, especially when so rendered because of the failure of our political classes to find a way to resolve their differences without resorting to compelling innocent and naive young men (and these days women) to do violence to each other as a solution. Once again the many are paying for the few; if we are still prepared to unquestioningly pay to subsidise the rich without seeing the absurdity of it, we are in grave danger of continuing to answer the call to arms to fight their battles too! ... **<u>Lest we forget!</u>

(Vegetable Pie)   *Fee Night 275/134*

Saturday 16th August 2014, Dunvegan, NW6-7 Showers, Day 669:

Yesterday Fergusons, [108] the Port Glasgow shipyard on the Clyde, went into administration. They are a company that made a number of ferries for the CalMac company.

Today has been a do little day mainly reading as the weather is deteriorating. We extended the anchor chain from 35 to 45 metres.

(Quiche and Salad)   *Free Night 276/135*

Sunday 17 August 2014, Dunvegan, NW9 Heavy Showers, Day 670:
Just under 241 years ago on Monday 13th September 1773 Samuel Johnson and James Boswell arrived here in Dunvegan and were detained here for some days due to bad weather. Unlike Johnson, who resided at Dunvegan Castle, we CAN claim to have "...suffered the severity of the tempest" and to have enjoyed "... its magnificence". [109]

(Tomato and Lentil Stew with Dumplings)
       Free Night 277/136

Monday 18th August 2014, Dunvegan, N/NW5-7 Showers, Day 671:
We spent today reading and listening to music and the radio as it was too inclement to go ashore or sail anywhere.

(Yorkshire Pudding and Soya Mince) Free Night 278/137

Tuesday19th August 2014, Corbost Loch Harport Skye, NW3-5 Showers, Day 672:
We left Dunvegan after lunch to catch the tides around Neist Point. After a six mile slog into wind under power we managed an excellent sail to Loch Bracadale and the island of Wiay when we had to put the engine on due to both dwindling light and wind. We motored the remaining 5 or so miles in what has to be probably the most complete velvety blank absence of light I have ever experienced out of doors; a perfect darkness.

Loch Harport is a featureless place in the dark and I had to plot our course directly from the GPS to the chart and cross reference it with the depth gauge and bark instructions to Claire on the helm. We finally anchored off the Talisker distillery at 1.20am local time.

The highlight of the day was being escorted for a while by a pod of common dolphins playing in our bow wave. One of them actually bumped into the hull of Drumlin probably by a mistimed dash across our bows!

There was a light rain as we trudged south east down Loch Harport; I am sure it was falling so slowly it was almost snow. Snow in August!

(Pasta, Baked Beans and Cheese)   Free Night 279/138

Wednesday 20th August 2014, Carbost Loch Harport, N/W1-2 Heavy Rain, Day 673:
I forgot to mention yesterday that in the morning we went up to the ruined church of [St]Mary's at Dunvegan and saw the same famous pyramid memorial that is mentioned by Johnson and Boswell. (A memorial to Lord Lovat.) *We also saw the Diurnish standing stone, a monolith erected to celebrate the millennium (this one!) but we didn't go all the way up to it.*

Other news - It appears that a British Muslim fighting for the terrorist organisation Islamic State has been on the internet in a video executing by decapitation an American Journalist called James Foley. It seems this atrocity took place yesterday.

James Foley was an American journalist murdered by Islamic State in revenge for US air strikes against them in Iraq.

The other item of news I want to report is that BBC Radio 4's PM program broadcast listener's sounds over recent months and these have been made into a musical composition called "Darkened Dreams" by composer Tom Harold. The work was premiered this evening on both BBC Radio 4 and Radio 3 at 17.50 hours by the Aurora Orchestra at the Royal College of Music and is a fusion of live and recorded sound. It was supposed to represent a traveller's dream recalling his/her experiences. It is a good concept well suited to the material. Personally I think it could have had more of an ending as it seemed, like a budget firework on bonfire night, to start with promise which ultimately didn't thrill and fizzled out in the end. The immediate response via social media to the BBC was mainly positive. It was a good exercise and was well concluded and rounded off by the producers of the PM program.

(Tuna Pasta)   *Free Night 272/139*

Thursday 21ˢᵗ August 2014, Carbost Loch Harport Skye, N/NW3-5 Fair, Day 674:

We were considering setting off for Canna today, but the weather forecast westerly wind backing NE! Veering okay, but backing means that the wind would turn right across our path. Tomorrow looks more likely although "Good Craic", a yacht we have seen before on our travels, came in at tea time and said how calm it is in here compared with the Minch! The forecast for tomorrow is slight to moderate seas. I suspect she may have been punching into wind to get here because we think we saw her moored in Arisaig earlier this year.

Much of the day has been spent reading, it was too rough to go ashore and the dinghy is on deck deflated. The dogs are a bit fed up, but it can't be helped. Hopefully we shall be in

Tobermory soon where they can get a good long walk away from sheep and near a pontoon.

(Vegetable Stew and Dumplings)   *Free Night 273/140*

Friday 22nd August 2014, Canna, NW3-5 Fair, Day 675:
An early rise at 7am saw us leave Harport by 9am, and we enjoyed a brilliant sail from Ardtreck Point all the way to Canna Harbour. By 3pm we were anchored in the centre of the bay whereupon we were serenaded by a lone piper at the small Protestant Church on the island who was entertaining a small crowd of tourists.

According to Haswell-Smith there is much of interest on the island, especially for me, as it has a good Viking heritage. Unfortunately we, like so many yachtsmen, are just using Canna on this occasion as a safe parking place on our journey to Tobermory. The next time we pass this way Canna will be a destination in its own right. Indeed I feel that we are missing out on the Small Isles as we have not really included them in our itinerary this season, yet they are so obviously not to be ignored.

(Vegetable Curry)   *Fee Night 274/141*

CHAPTER NINE

Dangerous Times

"This know also, that in the last days
perilous times shall come." [110]

Saturday 23rd August 2014, Tobermory, NW4-5 Fair, Day 676:

Canna harbour filled up with yachts and a couple of fishing boats last night. We were the first yacht to leave this morning and we had a good sail past the Small Isles (ironically named when one sees them up close!) to Tobermory where we had intended to anchor in Aros Bay, but it was too deep and there was not enough swinging room due to the fish farm and an onshore wind. We came back to our usual spot, but the holding is not good! Vigilance will be required tonight, especially if the wind gets up or shifts.

(Roast Vegetables and Pasta)   Free Night 275/142

Sunday 24th August 2014, Tobermory, Calm and Sunny, Day 677:

The night was still and the anchor held us although I slept in the saloon to keep watch just in case we dragged.

We topped up the main water tank with all our reserves as the 2 large 25 litre cans needed to be used and we have a couple of 10 litre cans in reserve. Oban is close enough for us to take on more. I also went to the supermarket for some shopping – we had minced beef for lunch! Protein!! Both of the dogs enjoyed a good walk too.

This evening we were once again serenaded by a piper aboard his traditional wooden yacht moored on the pontoons. What a great custom they have here of busking from boats! And to top it all, Claire did some baking making today a big culinary day.

I just remembered an amusing joke I once heard:

> *"Definition of a 'gentleman' –*
> *someone who knows how*
> *to play the bagpipes,*
> *but doesn't." [1]*

(Minced Beef and Pasta)   *Free night 276/143*

Monday 25th August 2014, Tobermory, E4-6 Sunny, Day 678:
It was announced today that Lord (Richard) Attenborough died yesterday; a great actor and the brother of David, the television naturalist and presenter.

Most of today has been spent wondering if we should stay put in this bijou anchorage in 12 metres depth with 30 metres of chain out or whether to relocate into a wider space and put 60 metres of chain out in 20 metres of water. 6 of 1 and half a dozen of the other! Eventually we elected to stay here as we are not dragging and the wind is not forecast to get any fresher.

The nights are noticeably drawing in now as the light fades fast at 9pm and reading becomes impossible, the anchor light is also having to work harder. We are into our last 4-5 weeks of the season now.

(Mince and Pasta)   *Free Night 277/144*

172

Wednesday 27th August 2014, Loch Aline, E/SE5-6 Sunny, Day 680:

There are F8 SE forecast and we thought it wise to vacate the confines of Tobermory for somewhere more sheltered and with greater swinging room. We left at about 8.45am local time and motored straight into the teeth of a fresh to strong easterly, that is Beaufort speak for F5-6, and spent the next 12 NM and 5 hours hammering into a choppy sea as wind opposed both tide and Drumlin. We arrived an hour before low water and the narrow entrance to the loch, which is only 2 metres deep and barely 100 metres to either side, was still crashing and swirling like an Olympic kayak slalom course. We ploughed on dropping from 4 to 2 knots as we crept in past the Ro-Ro ferry "Loch Fyne" and into the calm, serene, tree-lined amphitheatre of Loch Aline. It was as if we had suddenly been transported to another part of the planet as conditions inside the loch were totally unlike the maelstrom raging outside.

Sunday 31st August 2014, Cardingmill Bay Oban, S4 Fair, Day 684:

We spent most of today at anchor in Horseshoe Bay anxious to hear from our friends Nick and Jill as we were hoping to arrange a meet up as they were in the area. Eventually the call came and a plan was made to meet in Oban at 6pm. We relocated to the Oban's sailing club moorings at Cardingmill where we subsequently spent the night.

On our arrival ashore in the dinghy we saw a large wooden sign which had been recovered from the water and was lying on the pontoon. It was a Scottish referendum poster. A gentleman on a yacht moored nearby informed us it was an attempt by the "Yes" campaign to win over floating voters! It *won't be long now until poling day, 17th September, and then we shall know if Scotland has decided to remain under the rule of Westminster or if it has chosen to substitute one oppressive regime for another!*

We went out for a drink and then on to an excellent fish restaurant for traditional fish and chips. A good time was had by all. Both Claire and I were so hyped up that evening that we didn't sleep very well; that is how much fun it is to spend time with the crew of Amadea!

(Fish and Chips)

Monday 1st September 2014, Horseshoe Bay Kerrera, SW3-4, Day 685:
This morning's weather forecast on the internet shows a week of F1-3 winds mainly with a southerly component until Thursday, so Friday looks like the first opportunity to go south, but the wind strengths suggest sailing will be unlikely. We may just have to motor!

(Homemade Chicken pie with Potatoes and Broccoli)
Free Night 283/150

Tuesday 2nd September 2014, Craignish Lagoon, S<2 Fair, Day 286:
Given that the winds were forecast to be so light and in the "wrong" direction we decided to bite the bullet and set off this morning and motor this leg of the journey. We had a good event free voyage south arriving at the narrows of Luing about an hour after the neap tide had turned in our favour and we progressed to and through the Dorus Mor back to what is probably our favourite anchorage, Craignish Lagoon. We were snugly settled in by 14.30hrs local time and after a

bite of lunch and a short time reading I decided to inflate the dinghy to go ashore to post a letter.

Given that it was not too long before low water and a neap tide, the lagoon was unlikely to completely dry out to the full mud flat near the village. Claire insisted that she thought I would be able to reach the marina by boat and thus save myself the long walk along the road. I spent the next 2 hours trying to decipher the riddle of the sandbanks and shallows sometimes paddling in less than 10cm of water (4 inches in old money), but I eventually landed as the tide turned. I went ashore, posted my letter and, buoyed up on the rising of the flood, skimmed my way out of the quagmire like someone who looked like he knew what he was doing and had planned it all along!

(Tomato and Lentil Soup)   *Free Night 284/151*

Wednesday 3rd September 2014, Craignish Lagoon, E<2 Sunny, Day 687:

After a slow emergence from a very quiet night we ambled out of bed and began the day with a leisurely breakfast and a period of silent reading in the cockpit. I then decided it would be a good idea to take the dogs for a walk so I rowed ashore with the canine duo. I was really pleased to find excessive amounts of blackberries along the hedgerow, so I returned alone later to harvest some and made jam for the first time in my life. 300 grams neatly poured into an empty supermarket jam jar of 440 gram capacity. I'd made more jam out of the small handful of berries I'd collected than I had imagined I would; in truth about three times the amount I had anticipated!

The recipe I used was that suggested in Richard Maybe's book recommending simmering the berries in their own juice

175

for 15 minutes then to boiling with an equal weight of sugar until setting point. [112]

Once it has cooled I shall report back and whilst this is happening, Claire, not to be outdone, has rowed ashore to gather more to make a pie for tea.

A SHORT TIME LATER...

Well, Claire is back, the jam has cooled, we've tried some and I am basking in the glory of success! Lovely, fruity, tasty blackberry jam...

ANOTHER SHORT TIME LATER...

We have just finished tea and Claire's blackberry pie was delicious. I was struck by the thought as I ate these locally sourced, fresh from the plant fruit with their high definition flavour, that we are accustomed to fairly uniformly reliable, good quality food from our shops in our modern day to day lives. My imagination turned to the days when so much less of peoples' diet was so easily obtained and was more seasonally sensitive, and to how much a festival of delight that food like we were eating would have been to those who could not enjoy such delicacies all year round! They probably appreciated and enjoyed their food so much more for its rarity, seasonality and unadulterated natural goodness than we do today. I am also quite sure little if any of it went to waste either!

(Homemade Pizza, Free Blackberry Pie and Custard)
Free Night 285/152

Friday 5th September 2014, Craignish Lagoon, NW2 Overcast Morning Then Sunny Afternoon, Day 689:

Throughout the night we have been hearing thumps, bumps and splashes against the hull. This morning Gulls and terns have been crowding around us and we speculated that they were hunting the small fry hiding beneath Drumlin. By lunchtime the percussion had crescendoed and we found ourselves encircled like a cowboy wagon train in Indian Territory by mackerel, which were feeding on the poor little fishes! At first we did not think these larger fish were mackerel so I cast my line in and caught one straight away. Definitely mackerel! I let it go. Neither of us particularly like mackerel and we did not feel like eating fish today. It would have been wrong to take them.

> "I have no doubt that it is a part of the destiny
> of the human race, in its gradual
> improvement, to leave off
> eating animals..." [113]
> Henry David Thoreau

I took the dogs ashore for their walk today and happily met Pat the friendly local lady we often meet here. She was walking her dog and we had a stroll together and a chat about our travels. It is pleasing to make these acquaintanceships which are periodically renewed, and as Pat is good at noticing and remembering who visits the lagoon it is gratifying to be recognised, remembered and welcomed back.

We had half planned to go to Gigha today, but the wind didn't look committed enough to blow us along, so we decided to give it until tomorrow to muster its enthusiasm. Ironically we had fish for tea – out of a tin!

(Tuna Pasta!)   *Free Night 287/154*

Saturday 6[Th] September 2014, Ardminish Bay Gigha, NW4-5 Sunny, Day 690:

The BBC Radio 4 news announced at 8.30am that the parents of Ashya King, a little boy suffering from cancer whom they had taken to Spain for treatment as they had lost confidence in the treatment he was receiving, have, "Been given permission" by a high court judge to go to the Czech Republic for an alternative treatment! I am not sure if this is just lazy reporting, but "permission"! The last time I looked the United Kingdom was supposed to be a free country. Since when did free people in a free country require the permission of the State to do anything? Of course this is not some kind of Freudian slip; the fact is we do not live in a free country, only the illusion of one. We do not live in a democracy, but a parliamentary democracy; there is a difference!

"Democracy is the worst form of government, except for all those other forms that have been tried from time to time." [114]
Sir Winston Churchill

Most of you (As I do not live in a house I do not at present have a right to vote!) [115]*merely get to vote from a limited choice of a handful of people who will actually get to speak up, and they will be under the thumb of the party whips in the Palace of Westminster. Draw your own conclusions!!!*

If you doubt me and if you are British take a look at your passport. (Perhaps other nationalities' passports have similar wording, I do not know.) In the notes section, paragraph 6 entitled "Caution" it says:

"This passport remains the property of Her Majesty's Government in the United Kingdom and may be withdrawn at any time..."

178

The apparent freedom we so casually cherish is not freedom at all. We are at liberty, but not free. The State owns our passports and therefore controls our movement and may at "any time" withdraw that privilege. Those of us granted passports are effectively prisoners with licences to leave the country. We often think of our passport as a licence to enter other territories, it isn't! It is permission to leave our own!

This is a digression, but a necessary context in which to view what has been happening to the King family. I have no view on the argument they were involved in concerning the little boy's treatment. Those of you who have read *373 Days Afloat (and counting)* will be only too aware of my first hand experience of being in a similar situation with an ill child. We were fortunate in so far as we had every confidence in the treatment our son received and the clinicians who administered it. Neil had world class treatment from the very best practitioners, <u>bar none</u>. Not all cases are as straight forward as ours was; it seems Ashya King's case was not.

Brett and Naghemeh King [116] took their son Ashya from hospital in Southampton General Hospital against medical advice to Spain where they have a holiday home. It was their intention to travel to Prague where Ashya would be given proton therapy for the medulloblastoma, a brain tumour, which had been successfully removed by surgeons in July. At the time of writing proton therapy is not available in the United Kingdom for this condition. As a consequence of this the British authorities sought their extradition from Spain and the parents were arrested and held in prison in Madrid's Soto Del Real prison only to be released after the Spanish authorities found that Ashya was not in the great and immediate danger that the extradition request suggested! The dispute originated over a difference of opinion between

Ashya's parents and the medical staff concerning treatment to prevent the recurrence of the tumour; the King's wanted proton therapy and the hospital claimed standard radio therapy was the right course of action. The British authorities seem to have taken the view that the Kings were refusing to allow the child to have treatment and used this as the excuse to pursue a case against them. The fact is on record that they were not refusing treatment, they were just not agreeing on the type of treatment. From what I can gather at the time of writing Ashya is doing well after receiving the proton therapy in the Czech Republic and is in remission.

What I find worrying in all of this is the aggressive belligerence of the British authorities. We are living in dangerous times. Our complacency toward how we are governed and what laws are created is slowly drawing us into a situation where the State is able and allowed to interfere far too much in the lives of ordinary people. The scourge of political correctness and the contractions of freedom of speech coupled with ever intrusive and oppressive mechanisms of the State are eroding what little real freedom we have, and as I write this section of the book in late October 2015 I feel I should include here another more recent item of news that further underscores my fears. I am referring to the case of Karrissa Cox and Richard Carter who were recently cleared of child abuse at Guildford crown court more than three years after they took their six-week-old baby to hospital with bleeding in the mouth following a feed. They have been told that they are unlikely to be reunited with their child who was put up for adoption by the authorities before the case was resolved. It was finally concluded that doctors initially failed to diagnose the blood disorder Von Willebrand disease that causes the skin to bruise easily. The child was also found to be deficient in vitamin D which is the cause of infantile rickets.

Emma Fenn [117] of Garden Court Chambers, a criminal defence specialist with particular interest in representing defendants in child abuse cases, was quoted in The Guardian newspaper [118] drawing attention to the shortcomings of the Government's drive to speed up the processes of family proceedings and adoption. She also highlighted the lack of action being taken to stem the increases nationally in vitamin D deficiency and rickets. Furthermore, she was also scathing about relying solely on the opinions of medical professionals in cases where child abuse is suspected.

The tragedy of all of this is that it is nothing new. These travesties have been inflicted on innocent people by the authorities many times before. Let us not forget the Cleveland child abuse scandal of 1987 [119] where, thanks to the efforts of Middlesbrough hospital's doctors Marietta Higgs and Geoffrey Wyatt's use of a controversial diagnostic method known as reflex anal dilation, over a six month period in an area with previously typical numbers of reported incidents of child abuse, cases suddenly rose to such a level that social services could not cope with the numbers of children taken into care. The subsequent report by Elizabeth Butler-Sloss found that 77% of the cases were wrongly diagnosed!

Then there was the Orkney child abuse scandal of 1991 [120] on the island South Ronaldsay in which the children involved denied that they had been ritually abused in a Satanist cult, and where no medical evidence was found; still the authorities pressed the case. Later in court the Sheriff, David Kelbie, threw the case out because he considered it fatally flawed to the point of incompetence and that similarities in some of the children's statements were indicative of coaching. One social worker involved was Liz McLean, [121] she had been involved in the 1990 Rochdale Satanic Abuse case and also a similar case in Ayrshire. McLean was criticised in the official inquiry by Lord Clyde and in later years [2006] by some of the children she interviewed for the allegedly manipulative questioning techniques she employed.

Surgeon Dr Helen Martini, wife of Richard Broadhurst the island's retired GP, lives on South Ronaldsay and at the time of the allegations agreed to act as chair for the South Ronaldsay parents' support group. Speaking on 4th April 2011 to the Daily Record newspaper [122] she said that she could envisage such a situation happening again because of the poor quality and training of those employed in social work departments, child protection and councils. She roundly criticised the present day culture of box ticking and the lack common sense used in these cases. She welcomed the fact that training is given on short in service courses, but lamented the fact that the training is inadequate. Her conclusion seems to be that lessons have not been learnt and that although well intentioned, professionals are inadequately trained for the role entrusted to them and it is likely that other gross injustices will happen again.

(Vegetable Casserole and New Potatoes)
Free Night 288/155

Monday 8th September 2014, Ardminish Bay Gigha, NW3-4 Fair, Day 692:
I went ashore this morning to the shop and confirmed by asking the lady at the counter that there are more moorings in the bay! I was told that the original 11 are now 22 and that work has begun on the new jetty, bridge and pontoon. I also spoke to 2 other anchoring crews who share my displeasure at the squeezing of anchoring room.

I took the opportunity whilst ashore to seek out the 13th century Kilchattan church (StCathan's Church) and afterwards climbed the hill to see the Ogham Stone where I could get a remarkable panoramic view. I was able to clearly see the Mull of Kintyre, Northern Ireland, Islay and Jura. Meanwhile Claire spotted an otter swimming out to the skerries that define the seaward boundary of Ardminish Bay

According to the tourist information board this ruined 13th Century church which is dedicated to the 6th Century Irish Missionary St Cathan fell into disuse and became derelict in the 18th Century. A new church was built which is still in use near the hotel. The old church is now being preserved in its present condition as an archaeological monument.

(Tomato and Lentil Soup)   *Free Night 290/157*

Tuesday 9th September 2014, Ardminish Bay Gigha, Variable <2 Sunny Spells, Day 693:
Claire and I took the dogs ashore for a walk and called into the shop to buy another £2 loaf of bread! Like Ardfern, Gigha has an abundance of blackberries so Claire picked some and made another pie for tea. During the afternoon my terrier Chip "spoke" to Claire. Unsure of what he was trying to say Claire said, "Show me what you want!" Chip turned from her to stare at the newly baked and cooling blackberry pie. He was asking specifically for some pie. Naturally he was rewarded for his efforts later when the pie had cooled, and Bracken also benefitted from his companions clever interspecies communication. Chip has always been especially fond of fresh home baking!

Ashore we met a couple who had paddled past us earlier in an inflatable kayak. They came from Bendaloch near Oban. They came into the bay yesterday and anchored "Lara" next to us. They were based in Loch Creran where our friends Nick and Jill keep their yacht "Amadea". It is good to meet people.

(Lorne Sausage, Potatoes and Salad Followed by Free Blackberry Pie and Custard)   *Free Night 291/158*

Oscar Pistorius [123] is a South African track athlete famous because he has competed with medal success as a double amputee in both the Paralympics and the able bodied Olympics. On 14th February 2013 (Valentine's Day) he became famous for another less favourable reason; he killed his girlfriend South African model Reeva Steenkamp by shooting through the closed bathroom door of his Pretoria home. He claims to have believed she was an intruder and did not know it was her, nor did he intend to harm her. His trial began on 3rd March 2014 and ended on 12th September 2014 with a verdict of culpable homicide and he was given a 5 year prison sentence by the judge, Thokozile Masipa. [124]

Saturday 13th September 2014, Ardminish Bay Gigha, Sunny, Day 697:
The past few days have been spent quietly whiling away the time waiting for a suitable weather window to continue our voyage. Today I went ashore to buy some onions and to dispose of some rubbish in the bins. I took the opportunity to bring another 20 litres of water aboard and to take Chip for a run. Bracken is showing his age these days and is not always up for strenuous exercise. On the way over in the dinghy I met a couple walking on water. Paddling on surf boards is becoming a popular pastime, but it is a disconcerting experience the first time you see the practice for real; it is enough to persuade one of the evils of intoxicating liquor and to commit oneself to a life of abstinence! Once ashore I met another couple collecting water at the tap on the beach who liked Chip and were intrigued by how we live on a boat. The

main questions they asked were what we did for food and where we went in storms. Good questions too.

The weather looks promising for tomorrow so plans have been made for an early start.

(Lentil and Tomato Soup)   Free Night 295/162

In today's news there was a report about a man called David Haines. [125] He was a British Aid worker and father of 2 originally from East Yorkshire who was taken hostage by ISIL (Islamic State of Iraq in the Levant) in Atme, a village in northern Syria, in March 2013 where he was working in a camp for internally displaced refuges. He was murdered by beheading in the Syrian desert in September 2014 as part of a terrorist attempt to warn other nations, and specifically the British, not to assist the American efforts in the Middle east.

Sunday 14th September 2014, Ardminish Bay Gigha, E/SE4-5 Fair, Day 698:
The wind has a southerly component and would work against us if we set off for Larne in Northern Ireland today, so we have decided to wait until tomorrow when the forecast is for easterly or north easterly wind. The downside is that the wind will not be as strong, but if motoring is required it will at least not be working against us.

(Beans and Potatoes)   Free Night 296/163

Monday 15th September 2014, Larne Lough Northern Ireland, E2-4 Overcast, Day 699:
The weather forecast last night predicted easterly winds backing north east force 3 to 4 through the night to become northerly this morning. The fact of the matter is that it is variable in direction and blowing less than force 1! After a

long day at sea (about 12 ½ hours) we arrived in Larne Lough having sailed approximately a third of the trip and motored the rest using about 18 litres of diesel.

(Vegetable Curry)   *Free Night 297/164*

Tuesday 16th September 2014, Larne Lough, Variable >2 Fair, Day 700:

We slept well! This morning we woke up to misty conditions. I decided to inflate the dinghy and put on the outboard motor to travel the 0.8nm to the East Antrim Sailing Club on the opposite side of the lough to see if there is access to the shore and to get the week's provisions from the supermarket. Fortunately I met a gentleman there who let me out and subsequently back into the club grounds, and he made me feel very welcome. He also told me how I could come ashore when the club is closed and nobody is around to unlock the gate via a discrete public slipway situated just beside the club perimeter fence. This turned out to be very valuable information.

This afternoon I took the dogs ashore for a walk on the beach on Island Magee (Not actually an island but the long northward pointing peninsula which creates this lough) where we are anchored.

Now, as any woman will tell you, and any man who is honest enough will admit, men do the most absurd things sometimes. For instance there was the time when, not too many years before we sold our house and set off on this adventure, I decided to recycle the stumpy remains of some candles to make a new one. I melted the wax in one of Claire's best saucepans and, having succeeded in dipping my wick so to speak and making my candle, was left with a waxy pan. I was left with the conundrum of how to clean it before

186

Claire returned home to discover my transgression. "I know,"
I thought, "Put boiling water into the pan to melt the wax
which will float on the water allowing me to dispose of
it!" This was an excellent plan right up to the point that the
cerebrum part of my brain, high on the opiate of self
congratulation, switched off allowing my amygdale free reign
to tie up the loose ends. I poured the hot waxy water into the
toilet which promptly cooled the 2 immiscible liquids
solidifying the wax causing an acute onset of the plumbing
equivalent of angina. [126] This took some explaining!

I mention this because my lizard brain temporarily
grabbed the reins again this afternoon on the pebbled beach
where I was walking the dogs. I was semi-thinking about the
reason why all the pebbles and rocks were so clean and white
with black clumps every so often. Semi-thinking because I was
more directly wondering if the beach was manmade given that
it is so close to the Ballylumford power station. One rock
struck me in particular focusing my brain into one thought. It
looked like a leg of lamb in a butcher's shop both in size and
shape, but it was pure white apart from a flat surface on one
side that appeared glassy, like a giant boiled sweet. Just at
that moment my intellect made a brief return to the party.
Flint! I'd discovered flint. The beach was a "mega" lithic
deposit of what had been mankind's greatest resource for
about 200,000 years only falling from favour in the last few
thousand years. In that moment millennia of human instinct
surged through me and I sat down and began knapping until I
had fashioned a slice of vitreous rock. A tool! But surely it
was only a crude implement. I mean, how sharp could it be? If
I had to butcher a woolly mammoth what chance would I
have? The doorbell rang, the taxi had arrived, my intellect left
and I tested the edge on the back of my left thumb. Now
anyone who has ever experienced a paper cut will know how

clean a cut that is. Flint is THAT good, like a scalpel, so any mammoths out there watch out!

Claire and I went ashore to Larne at about 6pm and we were met by our 7 month pregnant daughter Hannah and her partner Gareth who were now living in Carrickfergus just down the coast. We enjoyed a meal out together in an American themed restaurant called "Blue Chicago"; an establishment that Gareth told us really annoys his sister Zoe because the decor is red! Well we are in Northern Ireland after all; things are bound to become funny!

Free Night 298/165

Wednesday 17th September 2014, Larne Lough, Overcast and Calm, Day 701:

It is my father's 75th birthday today. If I have one regret about this way of life it is that I cannot just jump into a car and go to see him on a whim. At least our son Martin and daughter-in-law Lisa live close by.

Last year we anchored here in Larne Lough on our way to and from Carrickfergus when we were visiting for Gareth's 21st birthday, but on those occasions we did not have an opportunity to go ashore. This time we have, and yesterday we had a close up look at Olderfleet Castle and a wander round the town. Larne is in fact steeped in history having been a port for over a thousand years. The lough is a natural sheltered harbour so this is little surprise. It is also a site of special scientific interest or S.S.S.I. and the western shores home to some of the film sets for the television series "Game of Thrones".

Olderfleet Castle [127] in Larne seems to be what remains of a fortified warehouse and watchtower, and dates from about

1612, but there has been a castle on this site since about 1250. The original castle was possibly built by the Bissetts of Glenarm, a Scoto-Irish family, and was strategically important to the English for the conquest of Ulster in Tudor times. In 1938 the castle was taken into the care of the state.

My trip ashore yesterday, apart from resulting in a small act of self mutilation, inspired me to write another poem.

(Sausage, Potato and Onion Gravy)   Free Night 299/166

Power Stations

In more reverential times
When mankind worshipped God,
He bowed his head to say his prayers
And followed where his Saviour trod,
And with the Labour of his hands
Built mighty temples where,
In those citadels of praise,
He cast off all his care. [128]

Those humble men their weakness knew
And sought refuge in everlasting arms, [129]
And called upon their loving Lord
To keep them from all harm.

Now, in this age, indifference reigns,
Man serves not God but greed,
"Gather more, as much as you can,"
This is the new Apostle's Creed.
The great cathedrals we now build
Are not for veneration,
The only force we call upon
Is power generation!

Once men offered up a prayer,
Before God placed their plight,
Today a finger on a switch
Is all we do to "see the light"! [130]

Andrew Dalby, Ballylumford, 16th September 2014.

On our travels we have seen a number of power stations including, Heysham, Hunterston, Tobermory, Stornoway, Kilroot and the colossal Ballylumford. Most of them are much bigger than any church and some even dwarf our great gothic cathedrals many of which took centuries to build. I began to think about our relationship with power, how our modern life demands so much of it and how causally we use and take it for granted. In this materialistic and egocentric era it seems to me our material wealth and ability to command and consume with frightening ease tremendous quantities of energy to serve our merest whim has made us become so comfortable and self satisfied that we are in danger of neglecting the spiritual dimension of life. For all our technological advances and material wealth are we as a species perhaps the poorer for it?

Thursday 18th September 2014, Larne Lough, Fair, Day 702:
Today is poling day in Scotland for the Independence referendum. Tomorrow we shall all know if we remain a United Kingdom or if we have been divided!

Hannah came to Larne today with her friend Heather and we met up for a drink in one of the town's cafes. Afterwards I walked the dogs on the flinty beach again. There is something about flint which brings out the caveman in me. I don't know what a psychologist would make of me, but I do feel the urge to both collect and "work" the stuff. Is it natural curiosity, something from what I have learnt and want to try, or is it something altogether more innate and primal? I'd like to think it is the latter.

(Chili Con Vegetables)   Free Night 300/167

Friday 19th September 2014, Larne Lough, Fair, Day 702:
Of Scotland's 32 council areas only 4 voted yes (Glasgow, Dundee, West Dunbartonshire and North Lanarkshire)[131]in the independence referendum. There was an 85% turnout and a 55/45% "No" vote.

The "Yes" vote total was 1,617,989 and the "No" vote was 2,001,926. Edinburgh voted 61% "No" to 39% "Yes". All the media news chatter today has been revolving around the Barnett Formula [132] and the West Lothian question. [133]

The fact that 16 year olds had a vote has raised the issue of lowering the voting age for general elections as it seems the consensus is that the young people of Scotland engaged in the process sensibly. My worry concerns teachers and schools influencing children and imposing their views along with the sheep like "following" mentality so prevalent on today's social media which could have too strong an influence. But it is not just the young now who use these media. Perhaps my natural conservatism on this issue is misplaced. The next few months will see wrangling over new powers for all the devolved legislatures, the decentralising of government, and the gradual federalisation of the United Kingdom.

Some statistics and ideas I heard today are that:

The English comprise 85% of the population of the United Kingdom,

191

That some English politicians are calling for some form of self determination for them given that the Welsh, Scottish and Northern Irish have their own parliaments.

London has its own mayor and other cities should follow suit.

Someone pointed out that the population of the Liverpool, Manchester, Leeds and Newcastle belt is greater than that of Wales and that it follows that they should have a voice, as should Birmingham and the Midlands or Bristol and the South West.

It seems to me that the referendum result means that united we stand so we can now fall by division!

(Pizza and Salad)   *Free Night 301/168*

Sunday 21st September 2014, Larne Lough, N/NE<2, Day 705:
I made a flint arrowhead when I went ashore today. I also cut my thumb again! It has been a pleasantly warm and sunny day and this afternoon we saw the East Antrim Sailing Club dinghy racing in the bay. There were a lot of Lasers and Toppers. Claire also saw a seal just after I commented that there did not appear to be any around here!

Monday 22nd September 2014, Larne Lough, Sunny, Day 706:

It is almost impossible to turn on BBC radio 4 and not hear the words "Scottish referendum" within a minute. It is funny how Islamic State in Syria and Afghanistan etc get forgotten...

We read, I walked the dogs and played my guitar, and I found some excellent videos on the internet about flint knapping. It makes sense when you see it done. Next time I am ashore I shall try again and hopefully, with practice, my digits will suffer fewer cuts and abrasions

Today I booked flights for Claire to go from Belfast to Inverness to visit her family and attend an Iona Community conference. It is crazy but true, that flying is easier and cheaper than travelling by ferry and train. It is also much, much faster.

(Vegetable Stew and Dumplings)   *Free Night 304/170*

Tuesday 23rd September 2014, Larne Lough, Fair, Day 707:

"Southern Cross" , a yacht skippered by a gentleman called Gavin, visited us today at 13.30hrs to enquire if we were okay and if we needed anything from the supermarket! We had met before further up the Scottish coast this year and we concluded it was probably in Scalpay harbour. Gavin kindly offered us the use of a safe mooring up the lough at his sailing club should the weather turn inclement. He has had a long voyage this year reaching as far as Orkney and Shetland.

(Tuna Pasta)   *Free Night 305/171*

Wednesday 24th September 2014, Larne Lough, Overcast and cool, Day 708:

A funny thing happened at lunch time. A police helicopter flew over and circled us once and flew off following the electricity pylons. Then another funny thing; at tea time Claire announced, "We've got visitors!" This is a phrase we often use when a vessel is approaching very directly i.e. one which will hit us if it neither stops nor steers away. Sure enough 3 very pleasant young men in a bright orange R.N.L.I. inshore lifeboat had come to our aid! Apparently we had been noticed, this time by "Concerned of Larne" who reported us to the Coast Guard. I told them that we were fine and that this was our 3rd time and that I was surprised Belfast Coast Guard hadn't telephoned us this time. However, on reflection this time the person reporting us hadn't provided them with the name of our vessel. They seemed happy and zoomed off again. I cannot be sure that the helicopter earlier was connected with the R.N.L.I. visit, but whatever, it was a lot of effort to go to over a perfectly innocent yacht at anchor! Claire suggested *that it may again be because it is getting late in the season and perhaps that is what drew attention to our presence. Otherwise it has been a quiet day.*

(Chili Con Vegetables)   *Free Night 306/172*

Friday 26th September 2014, Larne Lough, W4-5 Sunny, Day 710:
NB Parliament was recalled to discuss and vote on bombing I.S. (The self proclaimed Islamic State) in Iraq. I wrote in the margin of the diary "So it begins again!"

Sunday 28TH September 2014, Larne Lough, W<2 Sunny Spells, Day 712:
We had one last trip ashore with the dogs today and we brought the dinghy aboard and deflated it in readiness for heading out to Carrickfergus tomorrow. The rest of the day was spent in quiet contemplation!

Other News – Britain has resumed bombing Iraq and a conservative MP Mark Reckless has defected from the Conservative Party to the United Kingdom Independence Party (UKIP).

(Pasta and Roast Vegetables)   *Free Night 310/176*

Monday 29th September 2014, Carrickfergus Marina, SW<2 Fair, Day 713:
We had a very pleasant motor around the coast from Larne Lough to Carrickfergus today. We left after breakfast with a favourable tide which added up to 3kts to our speed for much of the way. We arrived at about 13.00hrs just at the start of the recommended 2 hours before high water so we had no problems entering the marina. (Belfast Lough is quite shallow and when the tide is out access to the marina is

limited due to insufficient depth.) *It was lovely to see dolphins in Belfast Lough and on what was to be officially our final day at sea for the year. The marina staff gave us a very warm welcome and we were soon settled into our berth when our daughter Hannah arrived. We spent the rest of the day with her and visited her in her new flat when Gareth came home from work.*

Having electricity I decided to unburden my telephone of the videos, photographs and notes I have made over the last few months. To my horror I found at least 2 poems missing. Somehow after many hours of tinkering I recovered them from an archive file on the device. How I achieved this I don't quite know, but I did and am very glad! Phew! Panic over...

EPILOGUE

It was meet that we should make merry, and be
glad: for this thy brother was dead, and
is alive again; and was lost,
and is found. [134]

Arriving in Carrickfergus was to be the beginning of a miniature adventure in itself. Northern Ireland is not the first destination many of us would think of as a place to find happiness. I suppose it depends upon what brings you happiness. For Claire and I it came in two forms, the birth of a child and a church!

Claire and I were both brought up in the Methodist tradition and just opposite the marina in Carrickfergus there is a Methodist church; naturally we went to check it out. It is unlike any other Methodist church we have attended. The minister, the Reverend Doctor David Clements, is a fine preacher, he has a gift for speaking to children and is highly respected and loved by the congregation, the local and wider community. The church members are extremely friendly and welcoming, not to mention persuasive; more about this later. Furthermore there is a weekly program of what in schools might be called extra-curricular activities that gives the place a constant buzz. Most importantly it is a place where Christian behaviour and values are present in copious abundance, not as a surface veneer or varnish, but more like a marinade which infuses those immersed and steeped in fellowship there and radiates outwards like the warmth from a fire towards any who care to approach close enough.

People who know me and have read my work will perhaps find it surprising that I like this place given my fundamental antipathy to The Church as an institution. I resent much of what The Church has done in the world historically and to me personally and psychologically, but I do have great respect for faith, Christian or otherwise, and believe that the greatest evil of all is to maliciously seek to undermine or destroy a person's beliefs. I grew up in precisely the Protestant evangelical Christian tradition exemplified in Carrickfergus Methodist Church, this context is my spiritual home, and as much as I love it, like any child I have rebelled, returned and redefined my relationship to it. Now, instead of sitting through a sermon and saying "yea" and "amen" and being satisfied to bask in the glow and comfort of salvation, I rage inside and argue and wrestle, not with God, but the Church and its teachings. In short I no longer believe and uncritically accept everything that I hear! But most importantly I do think, question, react and act. I won't let the, "God said it, I believe it, that Settles it!" argument stand unchallenged any more. It took years of disappointment, disillusionment in fellow Christians and the death of my child to bring me to a place where I finally discovered a truth, my truth. Once I let go of much of the received wisdom I had been burdened with, which on reflection was nothing more than indoctrination, I began to make my own decisions based on experience and what I felt and feel in my heart and know in my head to be true. I knew many of the ideals I had learnt were unrealistic; the religious disciple is very often set up to fail. Some traditional Christian ideas are indefensible (eg. The treatment of women) unless you accept the Bible as the divinely inspired inerrant word of God. I once did. Experience and insight has taught me that it is not. Christians and scholars can't even agree what actually constitutes the "Word of God" and which scriptures should and should not be included in the Canon of Scriptures that constitute the Bible, hence there are so many different versions. Do you remember my poem earlier?

"It is written", so we're told,
Brow beaten by pious men,
"In the scriptures, its The Word!"
Tell me!
Which god ere held a pen?

There was a time not too long ago that I was affronted if a preacher took as a reading a passage other than one from Scripture, a hymn or poem for example. Now I realise that other words, even those uttered in a sermon can be inspired words.

Sitting in church I often feel that God would be as uncomfortable there as I am, and probably even more annoyed by our misinterpretation or misapplication of the Bible's teachings, or by our failure to make our voices heard in the world as people of faith guided by conscience by speaking out against the atrocities and injustices society, the State and our leaders commit in our names. Yet in Carrickfergus Methodist Church we found friendship, sincerity and a place where people are accepted and loved for who they are, not who the formal church as an institution wanted them to be. A loving and none judgemental Church family is a rare and precious thing indeed.

Carrickfergus Methodist Church has a new modern building opened on 4th September 2010 after a 2 year period of construction on the site of the original church which had become unfit for purpose. It has been designed to meet the needs of the 21st century and it is high-tech, eco-friendly and capable of catering for the diverse needs of the whole community. In addition to the actual church sanctuary there are numerous rooms suited to a variety of functions including a full sized gymnasium, games and music rooms and a commercial kitchen serving a 50 seat restaurant. On Tuesdays and Thursdays 2 teams of unpaid volunteers open the restaurant and serve tea, coffee and meals to the general public the profits from which help towards the upkeep of this superb building. I mentioned earlier that the people of Carrickfergus Methodist are possessed of an uncannily effective gift for persuasion. Our first grandchild Ollie was born on Wednesday 12th November 2014 and the morning after Claire and I went into town on a quest to buy a cot blanket, but the heaven's opened. Claire suggested that we seek refuge from the deluge by calling into the church restaurant for a hot drink. We were given the customary warm welcome and recognised as the new people who had attended on Sundays. What conversation followed I cannot entirely recall if indeed I had much part in it. Suffice it to say that without uttering a word on my own behalf they had persuaded Claire to volunteer my services and I found myself working in the kitchen on Thursdays until we set sail the following April! In fairness to Claire she did also commit herself to what was to become one of the most enjoyable jobs we have ever had!

This new beginning in Carrickfergus brings us to another natural cadence in the unfolding melody of our sailing lives and it is a good place to return to the question which I posed at the beginning of this book in the preface, "Is this new way of life as good as we expected?" I can say with absolute honesty, "YES! For us it is!" I am not going to pretend that it is a perfect, problem free life, in fact many of the normal everyday considerations that beset us all are still present; we still have bills to pay, a home to heat and food to buy. The important point to remember, however, is that because our needs are so much smaller, because we possess less, because we consume less and because we live in a smaller space, the effort to sustain ourselves is greatly reduced and the time we have to enjoy being in the moment appreciating our surroundings is so much greater. We have learnt that levels of well-being, general health and happiness are inversely proportionate to the amount of energy invested in the pursuit of material things. We have really experienced the truth of the old adage that less is more.

Are we wealthy? No!

Are we Rich? Yes, beyond the dreams of avarice.

A nomadic life aboard a small sailing boat may not be everyone's idea of a good life, indeed for some it may be a terrifying prospect, but what our example illustrates is that a simplified life liberated from the clutches of consumerism allows us to see through the myth that fulfilment and meaning can only be achieved by the continual acquisition of stuff which necessitates longer working hours, bigger wages and increasing levels of stress and debt. All these things are a burden under which one slowly buckles and crumbles until we are burnt out and we have nothing left to give.

I have also illustrated in this present chapter how it is also important to divest oneself of some of the clutter and baggage that we carry around within us in our psyche. The burden of fear, guilt, shame, resentment and disappointment and so forth that constantly irritates our inner self and has literally found its way under our skin can be the heaviest, most damaging and destructive loads anyone has to bear. For my part it has been cathartic to forgive the younger me for his faults and accept myself for who I am, putting aside those things that get in the way. Thus freed I have been able to move on. Recalibrating our lives in such a way that we focus on what we need rather than what we want allows us to reconnect with what is important and natural.

Is this a recipe for happiness? Not necessarily, but it is almost guaranteed to bring about significant improvement and change for the better. Neither is it a onetime solution, but rather a continual process of re-simplification keeping things as straightforward as possible, a continual guarding against the seductions of consumerism and a continual reassessment and pursuit of what is really important to us.

Is it difficult to do? No. It is a process and it begins and persists with small steps. It is as much a state of mind as it is a way of life. There are no rules, just the uncomplicated notion of keeping things simple and easily manageable.

I challenge you to try simplifying your life and I am sure that you will be amazed to discover what you can live without and astonished at how much better you will feel for making such changes. This is not an unnatural ascetic doctrine that demands a life of self denial, hardship or even privation, quite the reverse; this is a life of plenty where enough is as good as a feast, and increased quantities of contentment our daily companion.

Appendix

Recipes by ratio

"To reduce a romantic ideal to a working
plan is a very difficult thing." [135]
Erskine Childers

Let us assume that the average person or family will
perhaps buy pies and pizzas, biscuits and cakes, bread, fruit,
frozen vegetables and meat in a typical week's shopping, and
that some of this will go to waste if it goes stale or out of date.
Let us also consider the cost of readymade foods and the
health considerations associated with processed foods. There
are a lot of factors that make this expensive in financial terms,
time and health or well being. Now consider a shopping trip
that buys food in its ingredient form; flour, dairy products,
oats, fresh fruit, vegetables and perhaps meat. Many of these
items will have a longer shelf life and are probably better for
us nutritionally. They are almost certainly going to be
cheaper.

As a general rule of thumb it is probably fair to say that
food when purchased is free from Value Added Tax provided
that it is not confectionery, crisps or savoury snacks, hot food,
sports drinks, hot takeaways, ice cream, soft drinks, alcoholic
drinks or mineral water. [136] Be careful though because 20% of
the money you hand over for those chocolate biscuits, crisps
or drive through hamburgers for example is being given
directly to Her Majesty's Revenue and Customs in the form of
V.A.T. Think about it, the pound you earned had 20 pence
taken off and given to the State in income tax, then a further
16 pence of the remaining 80 that you spent on those crisps
also went into the coffers of the tax man in V.A.T. You may

just have relinquished up to 36%, yes, over ⅓ of that portion of your hard earned cash to the State! Your £1 is actually worth 64 pence. And if that does not particularly concern you remember that this could represent slightly more than the first 20 minutes of each hour you spend at work when you will be labouring to inject funds into the treasury rather than your own pocket. Next time someone asks you who you work for, what will you tell them? And next time you consider how much you earn will you think of the amount you worked for, or the amount they left you with after raiding your wages?

Let us take a simple example using very approximate fictional pricing to illustrate a point about food:

Shop bought Pizza	£2	Quantity 1
Takeaway Pizza	£5	Quantity 1

Home made Pizza ingredients
Flour	£0.80
Margrine	£1.50
Cheese	£2.00
Vegetable Topping	£1.00

Total	£5.30	Quantity 4 or 5.
	Between £1.06 & £133 each	

We must remember that the ingredients for our pizza(s) will have been made from our store of goods which will contain sufficient extra produce to use in other meals. The flour left may well go into a cake, the cheese into a sandwich, and the vegetables used in the toppings will in reality cost pennies and barely dent our week's supply. The time spent making the pizza (roughly half an hour) is probably less time than you will spend waiting for one to be delivered from the local pizzeria. If you work an 8 hour day on minimum wage, a takeaway could cost you perhaps the equivalent of 45 minutes of your working life just to pay for it!

When we think about our food not as a series of individual items or meals, but as a more general concept it actually becomes easier to shop and cook. We are concerned with the 3Fs (FFFs); Fats, Fluids, Flour and sugar, and when we consider meals these often consist of a staple, vegetables, protein and a sauce. Once we have grasped the basics it is all a matter of how we combine them.

The recipes that follow use a measuring system based on a measure the size of a plastic shot glass which is about 75ml (or 1/8 pint) and about the same size as the average egg and holds roughly an ounce of weight (given that a variety of ingredients have different densities it is still a good enough approximation for our purpose). In fact I do use a plastic shot glass as my measure with very acceptable results! I can also assert with more than a small degree of assurance that these recipes will not see you winning a gold award in a baking competition or winning any prizes on a television chef's show, however, they will fill your stomach and those of the people you love and care for with wholesome fare without impacting too heavily on your time and bank account. I have not included oven temperatures; our medieval ancestors baked perfectly well without any type of thermometer. Just make sure that your oven is properly hot. I usually aim at about 75-80% of maximum. Experience will inform you, experimentation and practice will expand your knowledge of what does and does not work and using general principals will free you from having to submit to slavishly following the restrictive, prescriptive and inhibiting effects of relying on recipe books all the time. For example I have discovered that when I cook using these recipes I have found that my measuring cup needs to be used conservatively when measuring sugar and fats to prevent cakes crystallising or pastries from being too moist.

The basic ingredients are as follows:
Fats: Butter or spread, margarine, lard, cheese and suet.
Fluids: Water, milk and eggs
Flour: Always plain [137] and also oats.
Sugar: Also salt.

There are also two other important ingredients and it is helpful to understand their function. They are; are baking powder, which makes things rise, and bicarbonate of soda, which makes things crisp. To this larder of basic ingredients we can add our preferred fruit, vegetables, rice, pasta and meats et cetera. Tins of chopped tomato are one of our most frequently used ingredients for sauces in meals too.

Bread
Flour as required
Water
Bicarbonate of soda
A pinch of salt and bake.

Sauces for meals
8 (4) parts fluid
(eg. water, milk, stock, chopped tomato etc)
2 (1) part fat
1 (½) part flour
Herbs or spices to suit

Sweet and Sour Sauce
1 part sugar
1 part vinegar

3 parts tomato sauce or pineapple

Pastry
    2 parts flour
    1 part fat (I use 50/50 margarine and lard)
    A pinch of salt
    A dash of water for consistency

Dumplings
    The same as pastry but with a dash of baking powder
    Instead of Lard use suet instead

Scones
    6 parts flour
    1 part fat (margarine)
    A dash of baking powder
    Milk as required for consistency
Either
    1 part grated cheese (another fat) and
    a dash of herbs for savoury scones
Or
    1 part sugar for sweet ones
    Dried fruit can also be added if you desire

NB Scones are a good substitute for bread. Try having one with a poached egg on it. Better still, use a basic scone mixture as a pizza base.

Yorkshire pudding
    Equal parts eggs and flour
    Thin with 50/50 milk and water mix

Pancakes
    The same as Yorkshire puddings but
    only thin the mixture with milk

Sponge cake
    1 part eggs
    2 parts flour with a dash of baking powder
    2 parts Margarine
    2 parts sugar

Porridge
    Equal parts oats, water and milk
    A dash of salt
    Heat in a pan
Serve with sugar and milk if desired.

Armed with the ideas above it is a matter of a little imagination to combine them in various ways to concoct all manner of dishes. A quiche is basically an omelette in a pastry base. When I was young it wasn't called egg and bacon pie for nothing! Add some onions, mushrooms and peppers precooked to your beaten eggs and pour into the pastry base what would have become a Spanish omelette in a pan is a quiche. A little trick worth knowing is that a slice of bread crumbled and added to the mixture will give it a fuller texture. Cook meat pieces or mince with a few vegetables in a pan, set aside the gravy and bake the result in a pastry case you have a pie. Make a scone mixture, roll it thin and wide covering of tomato ketchup and grated cheese you have created a pizza. Add toppings to taste. The possibilities are endless. Bon appétit!

-oOo-

Have you ever wondered?

Have you ever wondered, or asked the question why,
When we think of Heaven, we look toward the sky,
Or when we think of angels, we think of wings that fly?

Have you ever wondered, or has it crossed your mind,
Why people crave for love, and want us to be kind,
Or why some others could care not less; and no one seems
to mind?

So why is Heaven up so high and only angels given wings?
Have you ever paused to think why we believe such
things?

We can make our heaven around us where we stand,
And rise on wings of love, fly kindness from our hands.
We can show we do care, and make this our Promised
Land.

So why is Heaven up so high, where are my angel wings?
Have you ever thought to ask for answers to such things?

I will make my heaven around me where I stand,
And rise on wings of love, fly kindness from my hands,
I will show I do care, and make here my Promised Land!

So; heaven need not be up high, and angels can keep their
wings,
I'll make my Promised Land right here, amongst God's
earthly things!

Andrew Dalby, Troon, 24th October 2013

This poem began as a song but I was not entirely happy with it and never set it to music. I felt that it would be better as a poem so I reworked it on 6th October 2014 in Carrickfergus.

I have long wrestled with religion which requires us to postpone life, always promising better things tomorrow in a better place somewhere else; in short, a reward after you are dead and gone! Religion, like the musher of a dog team, cynically and deliberately dangles a bone just out of reach in order to make the faithful content to labour in a futile attempt to obtain that which will always be beyond their grasp, and is guilty of causing some people to waste their lives in the pursuit of the impossible at the expense of realising their true potential in the present.

"... we should not postpone and refer and wish, but
do broad justice where we are ..." [138]
Ralph Waldo Emerson

Aphorism

"The only thing we truly possess is our life; we are not given it;
we cannot pass it on to someone else; we cannot replace it or be
compensated for its loss. It is ours, uniquely ours; the one precious thing that we have, and we have a duty to use our mind and intellect to protect it from being diminished or harmed. Do not, therefore, allow tradition, doctrine or received wisdom to pollute the purity of your own thoughts, to the detriment of your life and your living."

Andrew Dalby 3rd September 2013

-oOo-

The Next Beginning!

References

Chapter One

1   Sir Winston Churchill, Speech at The Lord Mayor's Luncheon, Mansion House, 10th November 1942. Retrieved from: http://www.churchill-society-london.org.uk on 8th October 2014.

2   Andrew Dalby, 373 Days Afloat (and counting), PublishNation, London, 2014, Page 168.

3   373 Days Afloat Op.cit. Pg 165

4   Henry David Thoreau, Waldon and Other writings, Bantam Books , New York, 1962, Pg 122.

5   Waldon and Other writings, Op.cit. Pg 154

Chapter Two

6   The Bible, Matthew, Chapter 2 Verse 9, KJV.

7   The Bible, Luke, Chapter 2 Verses 1 and 3, KJV

8   The Bible, Revelation, Chapter 5, Verse 12. KJV.

9   R. W. Emerson, Self-Reliance and Other Essays, Dover Publications, New York, Inc.1993. Pages 24 – 25.

10   Walden and Other Writings, Op.cit. Page 221.

11   The texts I set to music were from Psalms 46, 118, 122, 125 and 135.

12   The Bible, 1 Kings, Chapter 19, Verse 12. KJV.

13   S. Johnson, On the false use of the term "patriotism" by John Stuart, 3rd Earl of Bute, 7 April 1775. Retrieved from: http://en.wikipedia.org "Political Views of Samuel Johnson" on 8th October 2014.

14   Emma Goldman, Patriotism, A Menace to Liberty, 1911
http://www.spunk.org/library/writers/goldman/sp000064.txt retrieved on 3rd October 2015

15   Emma Goldman, Patriotism, A Menace to Liberty, Op. Cit.

16   See www.slspares.co.uk

17   www.troononline.net Accessed 6th October 2015

Chapter Three

18   Retrieved from:
http://www.rinkworks.com/said/murraywalker.shtml on 10th October 2015.

19   http://www.wateraid.org/uk

20   Richard Mabey, Food for Free, HarperCollins, London, 2012, Page 232.

21   The Bible, Luke, Chapter 10, Verses 30 – 33, KJV.

22   The expression "to swing a cat" is an old nautical term. A cat o' nine tails was a multi tailed whip used by the

Royal Navy to inflict what would now be considered by the European Convention on Human Rights to be inhuman or degrading treatment or punishment. Cat is also short for catamaran, a boat with two hulls side by side.

23   Samuel Johnson, A Journey to the Western Islands of Scotland and The Journal of a Tour to the Hebrides, Penguin Classics, 1984, Harmondsworth, Page 132.

24   James Boswell, A Journey to the Western Islands of Scotland and The Journal of a Tour to the Hebrides, Op. Cit. Pg 349.

25   Retrieved on 26th October 2015 from: https://en.wikipedia.org/wiki/HMS_Dreadnought_%28S101% 29

Chapter Four

26   Walden and Other Writings, A Week on the Concord and Merrimack Rivers, Op. Cit. Page 39

27   Retrieved 8th May 2014 from: http://en.wikipedia.org "MV Discovery" Also see http://www.allleisuregroup.com/

28   Retrieved from: http://www.combinedops.com/516%20Sqd.htm on 1st October 2015

29   Hamish Haswell-Smith, Scottish Islands, Canongate Books Ltd, Edinburgh, 1996, Page 106

30   Paul Sterry, Complete British Wildlife, HarperCollins, London,1997, Page 54.

31   Samuel Johnson, A Journey to the Western Islands of Scotland, Op. Cit. Page 39

32   Information sourced from: https://en.wikipedia.org and http://www.secretscotland.org.uk on 1st October 2015

33   Information sourced from: https://en.wikipedia.org/wiki/Special_Operations_Executive quoting Geraghty (1998) Pages 347 and 346 respectively, accessed 1st October 2015

34   This Wikipedia entry references "article by Matthew Carr Author The Infernal Machine: A History of Terrorism". Thefirstpost.co.uk. Retrieved 2009-06-01.

35   Michael James Collins was a leading figure in the Irish War of Independence (1919-1922), and a senior figure in the Irish Republican Army.

36   Popular Front for the Liberation of Palestine.

37   Samuel Johnson, A Journey to the Western Islands of Scotland, Harmondsworth, Penguin, 1984, Page 114

38   Samuel Johnson, A Journey to the Western Islands... Op. Cit.

39   Episcopalians advocate governing the Church by Bishops.

40   Someone who prepares people for entry into the church.

41   Retrieved from Wikipedia https://en.wikipedia.org/wiki/Society_for_Promoting_Christian_Knowledge on 30/09/2015

42   The aim of the Jacobites was to restore the Catholic House of Stuart to the throne.

43   An estate manager for a landowner.

44   The Bible, 2 Timothy Chapter 2, Verse 15.

45   Horace, The Odes, Book 1, Number 11, 23 BC. "Carpe diem quam minimum credula postero" - "Seize the day, put very little trust in the future".

46
       https://en.wikipedia.org/wiki/Knock_Castle_(Isle_of_Skye)

47   See E. F. Schumacher, Small is Beautiful, Sphere Books, London 1974, Page 26.

Chapter Five

48   This famous phrase, although associated with the Watergate Scandal of 1972 – 1974, is actually a line from the 1976 film about the affair called "All the President's Men". It was artistic licence and was never said in reality. Information source https://mediamythalert.wordpress.com/tag/follow-the-money/

49   Here is an extract from West Coat Railways website http://westcoastrailways.co.uk/jacobite/jacobite-steam-train-details.cfm

"Described as one of the great railway journeys of the world this 84 mile round trip takes you past ... the highest mountain in Britain, Ben Nevis, ... passes close by the deepest freshwater loch in Britain, Loch Morar and the shortest river in Britain, River Morar, finally arriving next to the deepest seawater loch in Europe, Loch Nevis!"

50   https://en.wikipedia.org/wiki/Kyleakin

51   The Highland Clearances took place during the 18th and 19th centuries and were often brutal and violent forced evictions of tenants who practised small-scale agriculture. The result was many deaths from cold and hunger and the devastating loss of Gaelic culture. Often blamed on the English it was in fact the hereditary landowners who were responsible as they sought to maximise the profit from their land and to exploit the cheap labour of the poor.

52   For further information on this subject visit http://www.survivalinternational.org/

53   James Boswell, The Journal of a Tour to the Hebrides, Op. Cit. Page 252.

54   Samuel Johnson, A Journey to the Western Islands of Scotland, Op. Cit. Page 78.

55   Haswell-Smith, Scottish Islands, Canongate Op. Cit. Page 139.

56   The Bible, Exodus, Chapter 20, Verses 3 to 17.

57   NB Augustus M Toplady, 1740 – 1778 Hymn "Rock of ages".

58   The Bible, Matthew, Chapter16, Verses 15-19.

59   The Bible, Mark, Chapter 7, Verses 32-37.

60   Welcome Anchorages 2014, Editor and Publisher Alistair Vallance, East Kilbride, Page 3.

61   Further information can be found at http://www.thecrownestate.co.uk

62   Thoreau, Walden and Other Writings, Op. Cit. Page 106.

63   Henry David Thoreau, Walden and Other Writings, Op. cit, Page 97.

64   Retrieved from: https://fr.wikisource.org/wiki/Discours_sur_l%E2%80%99ori gine_et_les_fondements_de_l%E2%80%99in%C3%A9galit% C3%A9_parmi_les_hommes/Pr%C3%A9face

65   Thoreau, Walden and Other Writings, Op. Cit. Page 97.

Chapter Six

66   A line from "Territorial Was Song" in a Mairi Hanbury Album now in the care of The National Trust for Scotland. Information source: Pauline Butler, Look out on Loch Ewe: The Tournaig Family's First World War, 2014, Page 18

67   The Bible, Psalm 46, Verse 10.

68   The Bible, 1 Kings, Chapter 19, Verses 9-18.

69   R. W. Emerson, Self-Reliance and Other Essays, Op Cit. Page 30.

70   A Dalby, 373 Days Afloat (and counting), Op. Cit. Page 132.

71   Thoreau, Walden and Other Writings, Op. Cit. Page 76.

72   Information source: Pauline Butler, Look out on Loch Ewe: The Tournaig Family's First World War, 2014.

73   Erskine Childers, The Riddle of the Sands, Penguin Books, London, 2011, Page 93.

74   Information sourced from: Steve Chadwick, Loch Ewe during World War II, Wilderness Guides, Gairloch, 1996.

75   https://www.gov.uk/protected-food-names-guidance-for-producers retrieved 1st January 2015.

76   The Bible, Isaiah, Chapter 40, Verse 31.

77   See Steve Chadwick, The Wreck of the SS William H Welch, Wilderness Guides, Gairloch, 2012 and Steve Chadwick, Loch Ewe during World War II, Wilderness Guides, Gairloch, 1996

78   Patrick Henry (May 29, 1736 – June 6, 1799) American lawyer, planter, politician and Founding Father. Retrieved on 31st October 2015 from: https://en.wikipedia.org/wiki/Patrick_Henry

79	Speech made in the House of Burgesses on March 23, 1775, in Saint John's Church in Richmond, Virginia. https://en.wikipedia.org/wiki/Patrick_Henry

80	Retrieved on 31st October 2015 from: https://en.wikipedia.org/wiki/William_H._Welch

81	http://www.ullapool-harbour.co.uk/about-us/history/

82
	http://www.scottish.parliament.uk/Gaelic/placenames P-Z.pdf. Retrieved on 5th November 2015

83	https://glosbe.com/ Retrieved on 5th November 2015.

84	Jeremy Fenton and Anna Welti, Prehistoric Roundhouses of Wester Ross and parts of Skye, Publisher Unknown, Please see website: www.wedigs.co.uk

85	Angus Macleod, Original document title: Herring Fishing in Scotland, 1998. Retrieved on 5th November 2015 from: http://www.angusmacleodarchive.org.uk

86	Angus Macleod [Op.cit.]

87	D Shaw, Ullapool and the Klondykers, Published by D Shaw, Ullapool, 2011

88	See http://www.gerrysmhughes.com/

Chapter Seven

89	The Bible, Genesis, Chapter 11, Verse 7. KJV.

90   Nietzsche used the phrase "God is dead" in a number of his writings most notably in a work entitled "The Gay Science". He does not mean the literal death of God, but rather a rejection of or indifference to God by society.

91   The hydra was a multi-headed serpentine creature in Greek mythology which grew two heads for every one cut off. As long as it had at least one head it was invincible. The vanquishing of the hydra was the second of the twelve labours of Heracles.

92   "Civil Disobedience" is the title of an essay by Henry David Thoreau. See Walden and Other Writings, Op. Cit.

93   S. Johnson, A Journey to the Western Islands of Scotland, Op Cit. Page 85

94   Rob Hume, RSPB Birds of Britain and Europe, Dorling Kindersley, London, 2002, Page 188.

95   Perhaps Leurbost a few miles NW of the grave site.

96   This was unclear but I felt was unlikely to be 84 years.

97   James Boswell quoting Samuel Johnson, The Journal of a Tour to the Hebrides, Op. Cit. Page 293.

98

http://www.aberdeenships.com/single.asp?index=100 840

99   http://canmore.org.uk/site/102877/cretetree-an-acarseid-a-tuath-caolas-scalpaigh-loch-tarbert-little-minch

100   https://en.wikipedia.org/wiki/Raasay# Population Retrieved on 7th November 2015. The pupulation has fallen from 194 in 2001 to 163 in 2011, a fall of 17%.

101

https://en.wikipedia.org/wiki/Scalpay,_Outer_Hebride s Retrieved on 7th November 2015.

102   http://www.ship-technology.com/projects/mv-hallaig-hybrid-ferry/

103   http://ec.europa.eu/regional_policy/en/funding/erdf/ Retrieved on 6th November 2015.

104   http://www.cne-siar.gov.uk/

Chapter Eight

105   Horace, Ode III.2.13

106   S. Johnson, A Journey to the Western Islands of Scotland, Op. Cit. Page 81.

107   James Boswell, The Journal of a Tour to the Hebrides, Op. Cit. Pages 291-2.

108   At the time of writing in November 2015 Fergusons shipyard has been rescued and continues to trade under new ownership of Clyde Blowers Capital.

109   Samuel Johnson, A Journey to the Western Island of Scotland, Op. Cit. Page 82.

Chapter Nine

110   The Bible, 2 Timothy, Chapter 3, Verse 1, KJV.

111   The internet offers many possible sources for this quotation and the instrument varies according to the preferences or prejudices of the person delivering it, but I believe I am most likely to have heard Ronnie Corbett say this. If I have wrongly attributed this quotation then I offer my sincere apologies to the originator.

112   Mabey, Food for Free, Op. Cit. Page 179.

113   Thoreau, Walden and Other Writings, Op. Cit. Page 277.

114   From a House of Commons speech 11th November 1947, Retrieved on 25th October 2015 from: http://wais.stanford.edu/Democracy/democracy_DemocracyAndChurchill(090503).html

115   Since writing this I have found that it is possible to be included on the electoral register if you use a friend or relative's address; however, be very careful if your friend lives alone as they may only be liable for 75% council tax as a single resident, but may be pursued for the full amount as the authorities will claim that you reside there with them. This can also happen if you use their home as a care of address!

116   Retrieved on 25th October 2015 from: http://www.bbc.co.uk/news/uk-england-32013634

117   See www.gardencourtchambers.co.uk

118   Retrieved on 25th October 2015 from:
http://www.theguardian.com/uk-news/2015/oct/09/parents-cleared-of-abuse-launch-legal-battle-to-win-custody-of-adopted-baby

119   Retrieved on 25th October 2015 from:
https://en.wikipedia.org/wiki/Cleveland_child_abuse_scandal

120   Retrieved on 25th October 2015 from:
https://en.wikipedia.org/wiki/Orkney_child_abuse_scandal

121   Op. Cit. Reference 120

122   Retrieved on 26th October 2015 from:
http://www.dailyrecord.co.uk/news/real-life/orkney-child-sex-abuse-scandal-1099361

123   Information retrieved from: https://en.wikipedia.org
on 8th November 2015.

124   In December 2015 the Court of Appeal overturned the original culpable homicide verdict and instead convicted Pistorius of murder, and in June of 2016 his sentence was extended to 6 years.
Information retrieved on 14th October 2016 from:
https://en.wikipedia.org/wiki/Oscar_Pistorius

125   Information retrieved from https://en.wikipedia.org on 8th November 2015.

126   Coronary artery disease resulting from fatty deposits; artherosclerosis. Retrieved on 16/09/2014 from:
http;//www.mayoclinic.org/diseases-conditions/angina/basics/causes/con-20031194

127   Information retrieved from https://en.wikipedia.org on 8th November 2015.

128   The Bible, 1 Peter, Chapter 5, Verse 7.

129   The Bible, Deuteronomy, Chapter 33, Verse 27.

130   The Bible, 2 Samuel, Chapter 22, Verse 29.

131   www.mirror.co.uk retrieved 18th August 2015

132   The Barnett Formula is a system the government uses to work out how much public money is spent in Scotland, Wales and Northern Ireland and is based on the population of each nation. It causes debate because some people consider it unfair as the per capita spending is greater in those 3 countries than it is in England.

133   The West Lothian Question (sometimes called the English Question) concerns whether MPs from Scotland, Northern Ireland and Wales sitting in the House of Commons should be allowed to vote on English matters when English MPs are denied a voice on devolved matters.

Epilogue

134   The Bible, Luke, Chapter 15, Verse 32. KJV.

Appendix

135   Childers, The Riddle of the Sands, Op. Cit. Page 187.

136   Retrieved from: https://www.gov.uk/guidance/rates-of-vat-on-different-goods-and-services#food-and-drink-animals-animal-feed-plants-and-seeds at 10.21 on 11/10/16

137   Self raising flour can be used in any recipe requiring baking powder and cornflour is perhaps better for use in sauces.

138   Emerson, Self-Reliance and Other Essays, Op. Cit. Page 90

Index of Photographs

Cover Photograph
Drumlin at anchor in Churchton Bay, Raasay looking towards Skye.

Index of poems

Printed in Great Britain
by Amazon